MYSTICAL EXPERIENCES

Wisdom in Unexpected Places from Prisons to Main Street

Jack Farrell

Park East Press

Copyright © 2011, Jack Farrell

All rights reserved. No part of this book may be used or reproduced in any manner whatsoever without the written permission of the Publisher.

Printed in the United States of America.

For information address:

Park East Press
The Graybar Building
420 Lexington Avenue, Suite 300
New York, NY 10170

Library of Congress Cataloging-in-Publication Data

Farrell, Jack

Mystical Experiences/Jack Farrell

Library of Congress Control Number: 2010936848

p. cm.

ISBN: 978-1-935764-16-8

10 9 8 7 6 5 4 3 2 1

Dedicated to

Nancy, John, Helene

and all who shared their stories with me

Contents

Introduction......v

Part I: The Soul or Spirit Survives the Death of the Body......1

Chapter 1. Negative or Frightening Encounters with Ghosts or Spirits......5

Chapter 2. Positive Encounters with Spirits of the Dead......17

Chapter 3. Dealing with Ghosts and Possession......25

Part II: Protection by a Higher Power......37

Chapter 4. A Higher Power Often Protects Us......39

Chapter 5. Why Are We Helped Only Some of the Time?......49

Part III: No One Is an Island—We Are Connected 53

Chapter 6. Separation Is an Illusion......55

Chapter 7. Interconnectedness and Healing......61

Chapter 8. The Dark Arts: Destructive Uses of Psychic Energy 69

Part IV: Welcome to the Mystery......77

Chapter 9. Our World Is Far More Mysterious Than We Know 79

Chapter 10. ESP and Paranormal Phenomena......83

Chapter 11. The Relationship between People and Animals......95

Chapter 12. Assorted Mysteries and Anomalies......105

Chapter 13. Making Changes for Emotional Growth......123

Part V: Techniques to Experience Spiritual Wisdom 131

Chapter 14. Shamanism—The World's Oldest Spiritual Practice 133

    Wilderness and Sensory Isolation......134

    Chanting......135

    Drum and Rattle—Rhythmic Stimulation......136

    The Journey to the Lower World......138

    The Question of Shape-shifting......141

Chapter 15. Exploring Dreams—The Royal Road to Unconscious Wisdom......147

Chapter 16. Meditation—The Queen of the Mind Development Techniques......157

    Zen......160

    Mantra Meditation......162

    Candle Meditation—Simple and Advanced......165

    Vipassana—Using all the Senses......166

    Daily Activities as Meditations: Eating and Walking......168

    Meditation and Other Techniques to Cultivate Creativity 170

Chapter 17. Autogenic Training—A German Technique......175

Chapter 18. The Heart Exercise—A Taoist Technique for Healing Relationships......181

MYSTICAL EXPERIENCES

Chapter 19. The Power of Place: Unusual Phenomena and Place 183

    The Star Mounds of Samoa......185

    Stone Circles and Ancient Cairns of Britain and Ireland 187

    Measuring the Energy......193

    Healing Energy at Sedona, Arizona and the Role of Geology......194

    The Role of Ritual at Sites of Healing Energy......195

    The Importance of Preserving Sacred Sites......199

Conclusion......201

Reference Notes......203

Introduction

Extraordinary things happen in prison. In solitary confinement, called the "seg unit," men are restricted to their cells twenty-three hours a day. With nowhere to go, some go out of body. Other men put themselves in a trance state and contact the spirits of dead relatives. Dead former comrades come to street-level dealers in their dreams, telling them, "Get out of the drug game." A few receive supernatural warnings which save their lives. Many have been frightened by ghosts. A man in Baltimore fleeing both the police and drug dealers he had scammed went on the run. He slept in abandoned houses, where he sometimes encountered ghosts that terrified him. When caught by the police, he felt grateful rather than distressed. Some murderers are confronted by the spirits of their victims. Another man used Voodoo spells that harmed two people.

These are only a sampling of the stories I heard during the twenty years that I worked in prisons, ten in a maximum-security institution and ten in medium-security settings. Throughout my career I also maintained a small private practice. My middle-class patients in the community likewise have rich experiences, albeit not always so dramatic as those of criminals. In addition to the stories of inmates and patients in my private practice, I have collected stories in a variety of cultures. The cross-cultural material shows that my conclusions can be generalized and are not limited to the U.S.

At one time I would have dismissed the stories of parapsychological experiences. My education had emphasized the scientific method, and I believed that anything that could not be observed and measured was unimportant. But thirty years ago something happened that changed my life. Because I am a psychologist, Elaine, a journalist acquaintance, asked me my opinion on ESP. I told her I was skeptical. Elaine said she was working on an article about a woman she had interviewed, Blanche, who seemed to have a gift. Elaine asked me to talk to Blanche and see what I thought.

(Here I should mention that with the exception of Blanche, unless it was already a matter of public record, the names of characters in these vignettes have been changed. Blanche has been dead for more than two decades, and I believe that instead of violating her privacy, my use of her name honors her memory.)

When I made the appointment, I did not use my home phone in order to preclude caller ID, and I gave only my first name. I did not want Blanche to gain any information about me before our meeting. On a Saturday morning I drove forty-five minutes to Blanche's home in a pleasant community on the Chesapeake Bay. She appeared to be in her late sixties. When she asked if I'd like a cup of tea, she reminded me of my grandmother.

We talked for about fifteen minutes before the session began, but she did not ask me any probing questions. Blanche talked about herself and said she wanted to learn Reiki. She also bragged about her children, especially her son, who was a high-ranking officer in the U.S. Navy. She seemed to relax as we talked, and I relaxed at the same time.

When the session started, her first comment was, "I see music all around you." That got my attention. The night before my favorite band had had a gig in Baltimore. They were on top of their game, and I had enjoyed an evening of great music.

Her next comment stunned me. She told me that I had two children, and my wife and I also had a stillborn child. Very few knew about that painful event. Blanche also told me that my mother had died, but that my father was alive. This was true. Next Blanche discussed some health issues I had at the time, and there was a question whether one condition would require surgery. She told me that surgery would not be necessary. This later turned out to be true. Elaine

MYSTICAL EXPERIENCES

did not know me well enough to give Blanche all that information, so I was convinced that Blanche did have a gift.

Blanche's final comment turned out to be the clincher, though not at the time. She said, "I see you're working for the state." I said, "No," and told her where I worked. Blanche said, "That's funny. I see you working in an office in a brick building with the state flag out front." I went away from the appointment believing Blanche did have a gift but that her track record was less than perfect.

Two years later the state of Maryland was looking for psychologists to take part in an exciting project to reduce recidivism. The program called for giving currently serving prison inmates intensive psychotherapy using a combination of behavioral and psychodynamic techniques. From an economic view, the program made sense. At that time therapy added $7,000 per year per inmate for a total incarceration cost of $20,000 per year per inmate; so, after release, for each year a man stayed out of prison, the state would be saving $13,000. I applied and was accepted. I took an office in a brick building. When I looked out the window, the pole flying the American flag rose to one side, but the pole flying the state flag stood directly in front of my office.

I had been skeptical about ESP, but when Blanche showed that she was aware of personal details of my life, she showed extrasensory ability. It was not a tremendous leap for me to accept the notion that some people have the gift of ESP, but I was baffled that Blanche had seen something that had not yet happened. When she had said, "I see you're working for the state," I was not aware of the program and had not applied for the job.

Her vision violated my concept of time. I still do not understand time, but know that my earlier assumptions about linear time were invalid. I had assumed that time marched forward single file in a straight line, and that events in the past, present, and future were fixed in their places. I could not understand how anything could jump either forward or backward on the line. Blanche showed me that time is not as rigid as I had supposed.

After my encounter with Blanche, I became more respectful and perhaps more empathetic when patients reported scary paranormal events in their lives. I saved my notes on these incidents, although not with the intention of compiling them for any specific purpose. That changed three decades later at an extended family gathering.

My cousin Jenny and I had gotten into a fierce argument, and we were shouting at each other. I felt guilty afterward because I like Jenny, and a few weeks earlier she had lost her husband, only in his later forties, from a heart attack. The argument was over spirituality. Jenny believed, and still believes, that there is nothing supernatural. For her, matter and the material world are all that exist. She does not believe in God, and believes that when we die our bodies return to the earth and the nutrients are recycled.

Both of us were unreasonable and less than polite. I had begun to speak louder and louder, as if increasing the volume made my points that much more convincing. Jenny, although quite intelligent and the associate dean of a college, ignored facts and used all-or-none logic. For example, because I believe that God created the world, she assumed I am a creationist who denies evolution and that I believe the world was created in six days. Actually, I believe the evidence for evolution is overwhelming, and evolution is one of the tools God used in creation. On another point she said that astrology has to be hogwash because the moon, although Earth's closest neighbor, doesn't affect anything. In the heat of the argument she forgot that the moon's gravitational pull causes the ocean's tides. Not that I am an advocate for astrology, but I grew up on the New England coast. We had to keep track of moon phases because tides ran higher than usual during full moon, and we had to be sure boats were well secured.

In the weeks after my dispute with Jenny, I got over my embarrassment and reflected on my own spiritual beliefs. I wondered which ones could be backed up by evidence. I also wondered what evidence a person with a materialist view might find worthy of consideration.

One source of evidence for my beliefs has been provided by my psychotherapy patients. A secret of my profession is that the teaching is not all one way; therapists also learn a great deal from their patients. In more than three decades of doing psychotherapy, I have become convinced that a large part of the world is spiritual. Some Kabbalists—for example, Michael Moskowitz—believe that the world is 99% spiritual and 1% physical. R. Buckminster Fuller believed in the same ratio of spirit to matter. I am not able to give percentages, but people who see only the physical world are like those who lack vision or hearing. They miss a great deal.

My patients have told me stories of their lives, convincing me that not only is the world intensely spiritual, but also that there exist four major spiritual truths and several minor ones. The major spiritual truths are:

1. The soul or spirit survives the death of the physical body.

2. We receive help from spiritual beings far more often than we realize. Of course, bad things happen to good people, leaving us to struggle in understanding why we get help and protection some of the time but not all of the time.

3. People are interconnected. Our thoughts and feelings have the power to affect others, even at a distance. This power can be enhanced by concentration and breathing in a particular way. Our ability can be used positively—for example, to promote healing—or negatively, to do harm and kill. The latter occurs in the dark side of witchcraft and Voodoo, but those who use this power to harm others pay a terrible price.

4. The world is far more mysterious than we realize. Time and space are flexible and not as fixed as we believe. Some patients have told me of events that I cannot understand without my accepting the possibility of parallel lives.

Friends have said that these vignettes or stories are only anecdotal evidence and therefore unscientific. I do not agree; anecdotal evidence is often the first step in science. For example, acupuncture was long practiced within Chinese and Japanese immigrant communities in the U.S., but ridiculed as superstition by the mainstream scientific and medical establishment. This changed owing to an anecdote, not a scientific study.

In 1971, James "Scotty" Reston, a respected reporter for the *New York Times*, was traveling in China when he had a severe attack of appendicitis. The appendix had to be removed. The operation went well, but on the second day after surgery Reston was in considerable pain from a distended stomach and pressure in his gastrointestinal tract. A doctor inserted needles in the outer part of his right elbow and below the knees. This worked. Within an hour the pain and pressure were gone and did not recur.

The *Times* published Reston's account of his experience on Monday, July 26th, 1971. After that the scientific community began to look at the clinical effectiveness of acupuncture, and scientific evaluations began in earnest. Now acupuncture is widely accepted in the U.S., and several medical insurance plans provide coverage. Prior to Reston's anecdote, any American scientist who proposed a study of acupuncture would have lost status among colleagues, and funds for such research would not have been forthcoming.

Drug discovery is an area of science where anecdotes are important. Whether they are investigating analogs of natural products or drugs developed in the lab, scientists want to hear stories that a particular compound was effective for people before they devote three or four years of their lives studying it.

The patients who told me their stories varied in socioeconomic level. As mentioned, for twenty years I worked in prisons, a decade each in maximum- and medium-security settings. Throughout most of my career I also maintained a small private practice wherein I saw more affluent patients. The stories I relate come from both groups, usually told to me because the patient was troubled or puzzled by an experience. Stories also emerged when I probed to learn whether patients suffered from hallucinations.

Weeding Out False Positives

In selecting stories to include in this book, I have removed those that could be explained without spiritual principles. For example, inmates can be manipulative and sometimes try to tell what a person wants to hear. Other times there is an obvious scientific explanation. The following stories are examples of those for which a logical explanation is the probable answer:

The Man in the Cell

When I first got locked up they put me in an isolation cell. After a couple of days I saw a dude in there. I'd see him against one wall, then when I looked at the other wall he jumped over to there.

While inmates frequently encounter ghosts in prisons, this appears to be an example of sensory deprivation. When the regular amount of sensory input from vision, hearing and the other senses becomes drastically reduced, the central nervous system stops working normally and hallucinatory images appear. This man was housed in an isolation cell for inmates with disciplinary problems or at risk of harming themselves. The cells are sparse, with almost no furnishings except a sleeping platform. The inmate had only four concrete walls to stare at. The situation is conducive to sensory deprivation experiences. People know when they have a hallucination as opposed to a spiritual visitation. I asked this inmate if he might have seen a ghost or spirit, and he replied, "No. That was just my mind playin' tricks on me."

Another example of a logical explanation occurs in this story:

The Face in the Clouds

My cousin lives in New Orleans, and right after hurricane Katrina he went out taking pictures. The clouds were interesting after the storm, so he took pictures of the clouds too. When the pictures came back there was a face in the clouds—not clouds that looked like a face, but a real face.

In this example the inmate's cousin was using an older camera, and the film had to be sent to a processing lab. Photographers who capture ghost images say the photos are semi-transparent or gauze-like. Since this was a real face rather than a semi-transparent one, it was likely that an error occurred at the processing lab.

The next story from an inmate is one of the more interesting false positives:

The Hag

Sometimes I'm totally paralyzed. I can't move and I can't scream when I wake up. It scares the shit outta me. I asked a lot of guys if that ever happens to them or if they ever heard of it. None ever did till I met this guy in jail. He was an ol' country boy from North Carolina an' he said, "That's the hag ridin' you, man."

I asked him, "What's the hag?"

He said, "She's a woman, a spirit woman, a witch. She rides guys at night, an' if she rides you, you can't move when you wake up." I asked him if there's anything I can do about it. He told me to say the Lord's Prayer before I go to sleep. I tried that and it helps. It still happens, but not as much, so you better believe I say the Lord's Prayer every night.

The fascinating legend of the hag is widespread in both European and African folklore, and this story shows it has spread to rural North Carolina. The legend is discussed in both James Frazer's *The Golden Bough* and in Robert Graves' *The White Goddess*. A scientific explanation of the phenomenon describes it as "sleep paralysis intruding into waking." The body has a protective mechanism which puts the striated muscles into a semi-paralyzed state while we are asleep so we do not harm ourselves during active or violent dreams. For most people this mechanism switches off when we wake, but

MYSTICAL EXPERIENCES

for some there is a delay, and it may take several minutes before they can move. This time can be terrifying for those who do not know the cause. Some people fear they've had a stroke during the night.

With one exception, I have avoided stories from people with serious mental illness. The woman inmate in "Glass of Water" has a disorder and suffers from auditory hallucinations. I have included the story because it has important implications about her companion.

Nonetheless, these days it is more difficult to avoid stories from mentally ill inmates. After the deinstitutionalization movement, many states closed their mental hospitals. It was argued that patients could be better cared for in community mental health centers, but the community mental health centers never emerged, and private treatment remains expensive. Many young men who are poor and have a mental disorder self-medicate with street drugs. This leads them into crime, and they end up in prison. The percentage of prison inmates with serious mental disorders is much higher now than in the early days of my career.

Most who provided stories had minor mental or emotional problems, or they would not have been seeing me. Many of the inmates suffered from anxiety or depression, which are common enough in the community but more so in prisons. Prison environments are depressing, and the dangers exacerbate anxiety.

The middle-class private patients presented a wider variety of problems in addition to anxiety or depression. Many struggled with emotional issues such as severe grief, marital problems or anger management. Employment issues, such as difficulties getting along with others on the job or inability to keep a job, can also be problems for middle-class patients. Since I am a psychologist and do not prescribe, I work in coordination with psychiatrists who handle the medications for patients with more serious mental illnesses. With the one exception mentioned earlier, all the stories come from people who are not psychotic.

Mystical experiences cause people to change and become more mature in a way that is analogous to the changes people make when they move from adolescence into adulthood. These changes are more clearly marked with inmates. After an out-of-body experience or a visitation by the ghost of a family member, inmates slowly become less impulsive. In prison they are less inclined to participate in illegal activities, such as getting high on contraband drugs or homemade alcohol (known inside as "jump steady"). They get into fewer fights and become more serious about pursuing their GED, or they take shop courses to develop vocational skills. Similar changes take place among people in the general population, and that is why techniques for spiritual changes are presented in Part V.

I do not wish to give the impression that I am an expert on spirituality or that I am schooled in a particular spiritual path. The material presented in this work came to me from many people, often from a different racial or religious background, and I feel blessed that people disclosed their stories to me. I do believe that their experiences have important implications and those people deserve a voice, so I am presenting this material as a reporter, not as some spiritual guru or teacher.

A secondary goal of the book is to show that what we refer to as the world encompasses a spiritual component. Carl Jung said that on some topics one will get more wisdom from a Swiss peasant than from a Ph.D. academic. This is particularly true when it comes to spirituality and the existence of God. In academic circles in recent years there has been a resurgence of atheism. In that environment some dismiss spirituality by saying that a belief in God and religion can be attributed to a single gene, VMAT2, which imparts a religious feeling. One of my goals in this book is to show through the experience of my patients—clinical evidence—that there is a real spiritual component of the world. We cannot see gravity, but we can see its effects. The same is true of spiritual entities. My patients who have had spiritual experiences know that the world is far more than just physical matter.

Part I:

The Soul or Spirit Survives the Death of the Body

The chapters herein relate stories of patients who reported encounters with a ghost or spirit, each encounter implying that the soul or spirit of a person lives on after the physical body has died. An anthropologist friend tells me there are few universals in her field, but that belief in spirits is universal and it exists in every culture. Not every person in every culture believes in spirits, but a belief in spirits is present in all cultures.

In some cultures, the belief is widespread. In rural villages of the Yucatan peninsula, Mayan remains the primary language and Spanish the second. Near Tulum, a Mayan man who spoke fluent English told me they do not have an expression meaning "dead people." He said their expression for the dead literally means "those without flesh." That is, people who died are still with us, but they no longer have physical bodies. The Nepal shaman Bhola Banstola has a similar teaching. He says that we should continue to honor our ancestors because they are still here. We can ask them for help, and we should thank them afterwards.

In our culture seeing a ghost or spirit is more frightening to those who do not believe in ghosts or spirits because it is so unexpected, while to those who believe in spirits, the experience can be comforting. Some procedures for dealing with ghosts are necessary, and that information is provided in Chapter Three of Part I.

I have included stories only from people whose emotional responses and body language were congruent with their story. Many of the stories are from prison inmates, and inmates can be manipulative. Because some try to tell what the listener wants to hear, I have rejected those stories that were not accompanied by appropriate emotions.

On the other hand, some inmates are transformed in jail. The poet Gregory Corso learned to write in prison. Others have spiritual transformations. A colleague, the finest alcohol and drug counselor I know, began as a criminal. He was sentenced to five years for burglaries which he committed to support his alcohol and drug addictions. In prison, his cellmate was a Buddhist. Andre became interested in that path and converted. He joined a twelve-step program in prison, and after his release he continued a lifelong commitment to A.A. Andre also enrolled in a university program, earning the degrees and credentials needed to become a counselor. He has had a long and successful career in the field.

Although not an example of meeting the deceased, inmates sometimes have an "out-of-body" experience. This occurs more often among those in solitary confinement, sometimes called the "segregation unit." Inmates can be assigned to these units as punishment for disciplinary infractions, or to protect them when they have received death threats from a prison gang.

To say conditions in solitary are unpleasant is an understatement. These inmates never get outdoors. They are confined to their cells 23 hours a day, allowed out but for one hour alone in an exercise room and twice a week for a shower. Except for the one hour a day, they have nowhere to go, so some go out of their bodies. This occurs more often in older prisons where the front door of the cell is solid, with only a small window for the guard to check on the man. In many newer prisons the front door is like a grille made of bars that provide a wider field of vision. Jack London's novel *Star Rover* tells of out-of-body experiences and was inspired by the story of a former inmate. London obtained the material in conversations with Ed Morrell, a man who had been imprisoned at San Quentin.

MYSTICAL EXPERIENCES

Inmates have told me they visited other worlds, and they were plainly shaken by the experience. I heard a rumor of one man who was making journeys out of the body to search for a missing horde of money belonging to a drug kingpin killed in a shootout. In general, I did not get many accounts of out-of-body experiences. It was my job to provide treatment or counseling, or to make evaluations and diagnoses. If a man tells me about a parapsychological experience that scared or distressed him, I can ask questions. It is not ethical for me to probe for material that does not concern treatment or evaluation. My job is solely to treat and evaluate.

Another problem is that most inmates who have had out-of-body experiences are reluctant to talk about them. They fear being labeled "crazy" and then being given psychiatric medication, which they call "bug juice." Even those with whom I have established some trust and rapport only allude to going out-of-body. The following story is from an inmate who was not in solitary. He slipped on a wet floor, hit his head and had a concussion.

Jeff's Out-of-Body Experience

The last thing I remembered was slipping. Then I was up in the corner of the room near the ceiling. I watched while they worked on me and put me on the stretcher. In the ambulance I stayed up near the roof. Then I slipped back into my body. That's when it hurt and I groaned. The P.A. [physician's assistant] said, "Hey! You're alive!"

Near-death experiences are similar to going out-of-body in that both show our consciousness or spirit is not as dependent on the physical body as we assume. Another similarity is that people change afterward. They become less anxious and have less fear of death. They do not become reckless or take unnecessary chances, but they are less afraid of dying.

The following story came from Warren, who received a head injury and a broken neck in a horrific crash. Fortunately, his spinal cord was not severed, although titanium rods and screws had to be inserted into his neck. Twice during the surgery Warren flatlined, but the physicians were able to revive him. After the surgery, when Warren regained consciousness, his wife came to his room and she said, "You died twice during the operation."

Warren said, "I thought something like that happened, because I was talking to Granny. I was really talking to her."

His wife became alarmed and thought Warren might have lost his mind as a result of the head injury, because Granny had been dead for three years. She asked the hospital chaplain to see him and see what he thought. The chaplain visited and asked Warren if he was close to Granny. Warren said, "Very close. I lived with her for more than five years when I was growing up." He described the conversation he had had with Granny during surgery.

The chaplain said, "You're not crazy. I think you did meet Granny's spirit."

Chapter One

Negative or Frightening Encounters with Ghosts or Spirits

Some people prefer to use the term "consciousness" instead of soul or spirit. But, regardless of the term, many patients have told me stories that have left me convinced a person's spirit survives the death of the physical body. There are huge differences in the way people respond to an encounter with a spirit or ghost. Many are terrified by the experience, while others find the encounter comforting, and it often leads to emotional growth. Of course, the specifics of the experience are the most important factor in determining the reaction, but cultural background does play a large role. The role of culture will be discussed later.

The stories of encounters with spirits in this chapter are of the frightening type, such as this one:

Youth Center

When I first got locked up they sent me to the Youth Center. I woke up one night because my bed was shakin' hard and it was about a foot up off the floor. I sat up to see what was goin' on, and *Bam!* My bed dropped down to the floor. No one else was in my cell an' I was so scared I almost pissed myself. I stayed awake the whole rest of the night.

One of the guards was O.K. and I told him about it next morning. He said, "It was probably one of them ghosts that hangs around this old place." My father died just before I got arrested and

I wonder if it was him tellin' me I better straighten up or he's gonna get me.

This inmate turned eighteen while awaiting trial, so he was adjudicated as an adult and transferred to an adult prison. In adult prisons older inmates call many young men his age "hoppers" because they are anxious, have high energy levels, and move so quickly they seem to be hopping around. This man was not a hopper. The experience had a sobering effect on him. He also had factors that predict against recidivism. He did not have a lengthy history of juvenile crime, but he succumbed to the temptation to make fast money in a drug deal that went bad. He had a father in the home while he was growing up who was a positive role model, and the young man had a job which he held for a year. Hopefully he learned a lesson and will not be going back to jail.

It might seem impossible that a spirit or ghost could have the power to raise and shake a bed, but that is what the man reported. Another example of ghosts having physical power came from Stefan, an athletic Ph.D. student. Stefan enjoyed backpacking and sometimes went into the mountains alone. During a hike at high elevation in the Sierras, the weather turned stormy. He wasn't relishing the idea of sleeping in his small backpacking tent in a storm, when he spotted an abandoned miner's cabin. The cabin had a bunk where he unrolled his sleeping bag and lay down for a rest. The ghost of an old miner appeared and yelled at him, "This is mine. Get out of here." Stefan did not move, and the miner kicked him. Stefan had experienced ghosts several times in his life, so he was less frightened than most. He stayed in the cabin through the storm, which lasted all night. When Stefan checked the next morning, he found a bruise on his hip where he had been kicked.

Grant Wilson, who co-founded the TV show *Ghost Hunters* with Jason Hawes, has said that the people who investigate suspected hauntings for his show have been "punched, slapped, and

MYSTICAL EXPERIENCES

grabbed." In coaching his investigators, Wilson tells them that it will happen and warns them, "Be prepared for it."

The next story was told by an inmate with a long history of serious criminal behavior. He was serving a lengthy sentence because he impulsively shot and killed a woman clerk who did not resist when he robbed a store.

Dark Shadow

After I got locked up on this murder charge, I'd see this thing like a dark shadow flyin' by. I got scared because I thought it was the ghost of the lady I killed. My grandmother knows a lot about ghosts and shit, so I asked her. She said, "It's just a spirit, it can't hurt you. Don't pay attention to it." It's hard not to pay attention because almost every night I dream about the lady I killed. She comes to me askin', "Why?" Her face looks the way it did when she was in the process of gettin' killed.

This inmate admitted he killed his victim, which is a step in the right direction, but he continued to be in some denial of his culpability. He said "when she was in the process of getting killed" rather than *when I killed her*. An important measure of psychological growth among inmates is whether or not they take full responsibility for their actions. This inmate had more work to do, but unfortunately he was transferred to another prison.

To stop unwanted dreams from the spirit of a victim, a man must do several things. First, he must take full responsibility. Next, he must do some painful introspection, exploring the origins of his anger and impulsiveness. This usually requires the help of a therapist. Finally, he must enter a trance state and try to encounter the spirit of the victim. Then he must try to answer "why?" and ask to be forgiven.

Most prisons have a number of ghosts owing to all the inmates who died there, and sometimes murderers are confronted by the spirits of their victims. There are occasional killings, a greater number of suicides, and also deaths from natural causes. Inmates tend to die young because the criminal lifestyle is tough on the body. People with the ability to see or photograph ghosts say that one of the most haunted places in America is the Eastern State Penitentiary in Philadelphia. It is no longer used as a prison, and tours can be arranged. In addition to prisons, most battlefield sites are haunted.

In our culture, for most people an encounter with a ghost is frightening. My private practice is in western Maryland, not far from the Civil War battlefield at Antietam, where the bloodiest single day of battle in American history took place. A middle-aged college professor lives on the major road the Confederate army used to retreat back to Virginia after the battle. Many of the soldiers in the retreat were grievously wounded and died along the way. The professor told me he and his wife had to change rooms with their twelve-year-old daughter because her room faced the street. Although the battle had been fought more than 140 years earlier, when she got up during the night she often saw the ghosts of fallen soldiers, which terrified her. After her parents switched rooms with her, she could not see the ghosts. The professor would spot one occasionally, but he was not terrified like his daughter.

Wayne, a young man from Boonsboro, Maryland, told of remarkable experiences with ghosts a few miles from that professor's home. He was raised by his grandparents in a stone house that predated the Civil War, although modern plumbing and electricity had been installed. Frequently the windows would become unlatched, even on the second floor, and often the faucet in the bathtub would turn on when no one was in that room. This terrified Wayne as a child, but his grandfather asked him, "Have you ever heard of anybody killed by a ghost?" Wayne answered no. His grandfather said, "That's right. It's the living, not the dead that can kill you. That's who you have to be careful of." This did reassure Wayne, and he no longer feared the mischievous ghost.

Similar events have occurred at many battlefield sites. Soldiers killed in battle are usually young men who were not expecting death,

MYSTICAL EXPERIENCES

and so they are not prepared. People who visit Gettysburg often find semi-transparent spectral forms in their photos taken at dusk. Photographers who specialize in this work say that the Civil War battlefield at the Monocacy River in Maryland is among the most ghost-laden.

The Battle of the Monocacy was strategically important because it saved the city of Washington. To attack Washington, and take pressure off Lee's army in Virginia, the Confederate general Jubal A. Early marched 14,000 men north through the Shenandoah Valley and crossed the Potomac into Maryland in July 1864. An interesting aside is that Early threatened to plunder several cities and towns unless they bought him off. He demanded $200,000 from the city of Frederick, which had to borrow the money from banks to avoid destruction. The sum was huge for that era. The city did not finish paying off the loan until 1953.

General Early led his army toward Washington, planning to attack the city from the northwest. The Union army put together a small force under Gen. Lew Wallace. (After the war he authored *Ben Hur.*) Hopelessly outnumbered three to one, Wallace tried to stop Early near the Monocacy River. Although Wallace lost the battle, his men fought well and delayed the Confederates long enough that the Union army was able to send reinforcements to defend Washington. General Early realized he could not overcome those forces and retreated back to Virginia

About 2,200 men were lost in the battle, and now many ghosts are reported there. The photographer C.R. Angleberger heard a group of soldiers walk by his tent while camping at the site. A motorcyclist stopped to make some adjustments and saw a man in the nearby field. At first he thought it was a farmer carrying a shovel, but when he looked more closely, he saw it was a Confederate soldier with a musket. Another visitor saw a group of five Union soldiers pass through a fence as if it did not exist. Photographer Tracy Manseau said that many of her photos taken there contain "orbs" or energy balls of light. She believes these are spirits of the dead.

Some skeptics claim these are only reflections, but Angleberger and Manseau are professional photographers who are far more knowledgeable about reflected light than the skeptics.

Similar reports come from many World War II battlefields. A U.S. officer who had been stationed in Okinawa in the 1960s told me that once he and a friend had taken a drive into the mountains in the countryside. When they stopped for food on the way back to the city, an older woman asked them for a ride. She got in the back seat, but when they approached the city he turned and looked, and she was not there.

Disembodied voices have been heard at the site of many disasters. Florida divers hunting treasure have reported voices near shipwrecks. Guards protecting the site of the 9/11 tragedy reported voices of the deceased during the night. The writer Paul Watkins told of an unsettling experience when he camped overnight in the Ardennes forest on the Belgian-German border. That area was the site of the Battle of the Bulge, where some of the most vicious fighting in World War II took place. The battle lasted for a month, and more than 18,000 American soldiers were casualties. Watkins woke during the night, and he was certain that deceased soldiers were calling to him.

Of course, the experience of ghosts is not limited to battlefields. Juan, a young photographer from Puerto Rico, told me that he visited some members of his extended family in North Carolina and took photos. The photos revealed wispy, vaguely human forms among his family.

I heard the following story from multiple sources when I worked at a military base. This base had not been the scene of battles, and I continue to be puzzled by the story:

The Headless Woman of Hunter-Liggett

In the late 1960s there was a mysterious chain of events at a U.S. Army base, Hunter-Liggett Military Reservation in California. The remote base covers a large swath of land on the eastern slope

MYSTICAL EXPERIENCES

of the Santa Lucia Mountains. The verdant Big Sur coast sits on the western slope, but much of the moisture does not clear the mountains. The land on post is semi-arid and rugged. I never spotted a cougar, but sometimes saw tracks.

The Army used the post for wargames and to test prototypes of equipment under field conditions. Computers were needed, but in the 1960s and they were much larger than they are today. Those computers required generators and cooling. Rather than bring this gear from the main base to the test site each day, it was often housed on site in a trailer and left there for the duration of the test. A soldier was stationed to guard it at night and over weekends, but in those pre-terrorism days the soldier was issued a rifle, yet no ammo.

Usually this duty lasted four hours, after which the soldier would be replaced by another man, but standard Army procedure requires a man to remain at his post until properly relieved. One afternoon at 4:00 p.m. a young soldier was assigned to guard a trailer in a distant area where the post abutted the Los Padres National Forest. He had plenty of water and food, C-rations at that time, and a rifle without ammo. At 8:00 p.m. his replacement did not arrive, nor did one arrive at midnight. There had been a glitch at the main post, and someone neglected to order replacements every four hours. The soldier was annoyed that he was not relieved. And he was scared. The howls of coyotes echoed through the darkness, and he had no ammo if he needed to protect himself.

Around 3:00 a.m. a pretty young woman walked out from the trees and began talking with him. He assumed she was a camper in the national forest and had been attracted by his lantern. He was delighted to have company, and he enjoyed talking with her. After they had talked for several minutes, in mid-sentence she reached up, lifted her head from her shoulders, and placed it under her arm. He ran nine miles in the darkness over rugged terrain, through forest and thorny scrub, until he reached the main post.

He was lacerated and bruised so badly that he had to be hospitalized. While working at the post, I became convinced that the terrified soldier was not lying; he believed what he reported. Could his visitor have been a ghost?

Latino people had settled in that area when California was ruled by Spain and later when it was ruled by Mexico. The U.S. took possession after the Mexican-American war in 1848. Law enforcement was spotty in the mid 1800s in the West, and it was almost non-existent when the victims were Native American or Latino. In that area of California, authorities turned a blind eye when ranchers burned out Latino homesteads and took over the land for cattle grazing. If the apparition was a ghost, she could have been from that era.

The soldier's experience started a string of problems at the base. Rumors ran wild. Several soldiers claimed to have seen the headless woman, and there was fear among the men. Others used it as an excuse. Two guys said they saw the headless woman in the road, and it was that which caused them to swerve and have an accident. Actually, they wrecked their jeep while drunk. Finally, orders came down from base authorities that the headless woman was not to be mentioned. Enlisted men who talked about the headless woman found themselves transferred to undesirable locations, and officers did not get promoted. These measures put a quick stop to talk about the headless woman.

Although the bulk of my training has been in psychology, I have also studied some anthropology, and I know that ghosts are greatly feared in Samoa. I was also curious about the controversies in the social sciences about the transition from adolescence to adulthood in that culture. For those reasons I made a trip to Samoa in 2007.

In her classic study *Coming of Age in Samoa*, Margaret Mead said that the fear of ghosts, or *aitu*, reduced the amount of sexual activity. Young women were often too afraid of ghosts to sneak out at night to meet their male paramours "under the palm trees." Mead

MYSTICAL EXPERIENCES

said that the Samoans she studied believed that ghosts could strangle a person or "leap upon their back and could not be shaken off." According to Mead, the young men also feared ghosts but nevertheless waited among the palms for girls who were often too scared to show up.

When the U.S. National Park Service evaluated sites in the 1980s to establish the U.S. National Park of American Samoa, the people on the island of Ofu warned the planners to avoid the beach at To'aga because of deadly *aitu*. The U.S. Public Health Service had built a dispensary in the area of To'aga beach because it was accessible to people from both the islands of Ofu and Olosega. Despite the convenient location, no one went to the dispensary until it was moved to Ofu village.

When I was in Samoa in 2007, Daphne, a woman on the island of Upolu in nearby independent Samoa, told me that now the greatest fear is from spirits of deceased relatives who might attack because they felt disrespected by a person during life. Those spirits of the deceased might seek revenge for the prior disrespect by creating havoc among the living.

This fear of spirits of the dead is not limited to Samoa. It exists on all the widespread Polynesian islands, but people of Rapa Nui, or Easter Island, have developed a counter measure, a talisman or sculpture that protects against any spirits with malicious intent. It is called a *moko* and looks like a humanoid lizard. The islanders believe that malicious spirits cannot come within fifty meters of a *moko*. I bought one while on the island, but a man told me that since my carving did not have eyes, it had no *mana*, or spiritual power, and therefore could not repel ghosts. I went back to the carver, who applied eyes made from shell and obsidian, and I am told that my statue now has *mana*.

There is a similar fear of evil spirits among the Inuit. Peter Freuchen was a Danish physician and explorer who married a Greenland Inuit woman. They lived among her people for eleven years until her untimely death. He paid a price for his time in the

Arctic. After being caught in a fierce storm, he developed frostbite in one leg. Gangrene set in, and the leg had to be amputated. Freuchen reported that the fear of evil spirits became severe when winter approached. At that time people felt there was an aura of evil lurking around the village. He said:

> Every year, in the fall, we had a veritable epidemic of evil spirits materializing among the houses when the storms and darkness set in, and panic ensued. Sometimes nerves would reach the limit of endurance, consciousness would be canceled out, and the individual in question would become senseless and hysterical, doing and saying incomprehensible things.

It is interesting to contrast the attitude toward ghosts in the Polynesian and Inuit cultures with another culture where ghosts are not so feared. In traditional Irish culture, ghosts appear in folksongs such as "Molly Malone" and "She Moves Through the Fair." In Ireland people are not surprised when they encounter a ghost. The following story was told by Michael, an Irish-American tourist who was staying at a bed and breakfast on the River Shannon.

Did You See the Englishman?

A light mist was falling, but I wanted to go for a walk before breakfast. I grabbed my Gore-Tex jacket and asked the lady who ran the place about walks with good views of the river. She told me about a couple of places, and I headed out. Views along the river were stunning, and I saw lots of wild ducks and geese. Not many people were around, but one guy walking along the river was dressed like he was going fishing. I said, "Good morning," but he didn't answer. He had his head down and he kept going.

When I got back to the B and B, in a matter-of-fact tone the lady asked me, "Did you see the Englishman?" I described the guy, and she said that I had seen the Englishman. She said that he had come to the area for fishing some years ago, but he was terribly sad and had lost all hope. He drowned himself in the river. Now his ghost wanders the banks, especially on rainy days when few people are around.

Those who are convinced that matter and material forces are all that exist have a difficult time explaining encounters with ghosts or spirits. They believe that when we die, our bodies decompose and return to the earth, and that is it. Our consciousness ends with the death of the body. These stories of ghosts indicate that the spirit lives on, although the particular experience might be shaped by the cultural context.

Chapter Two

Positive Encounters with Spirits of the Dead

Surprisingly, many stories of encounters with spirits are positive rather than negative. As the Polynesian and contrasting Irish views demonstrate, cultural factors have a role in determining the quality of the experience. On November 1st Mexicans honor their dead relatives during *La Día de los Muertos*, or the Day of the Dead. The family may go to the cemetery or set up an altar in the home where pictures of the dead are placed, as well as the favorite foods and drinks of the deceased.

This is an ancient festival, going back to peoples who preceded the Aztecs and populated the region long before the coming of the Spanish. As one Mexican-American told me, "We're not afraid of spirits. We party with them." Of course, the specifics of the experience have a role in determining whether an encounter with a spirit is positive or negative.

The next story was told by an African-American inmate from a rural area on Maryland's Eastern Shore:

Father and Brother

My father died when I was eleven—heart failure. My brother got killed when I was fifteen. One of his friends was smokin' PCP, zapped out and just stabbed him up. Now my brother comes to me in my dreams. He tells me he's O.K., and don't worry. Things will work out for me when I get out of jail. Once he told me he loved me, but most of the time it's just like when he was home. We sit around chillin'.

When I need to, like I'm feelin' lonely or want advice, I talk to my father. First I do something to put myself in a zone, like stare at my cigarette lighter. Then I can talk to my father. Sometimes it feels like it's all in my head, like I'm talkin' to myself. Other times I get good advice or hear stuff I didn't know before. Last week I was the only guy on the tier who knew we were gonna have that shakedown on Thursday.

His brother told the young man that he is O.K., and not to worry because things will work out for him after he gets out of jail. These are significant statements. Such reassurances are the most frequent content I hear from patients who tell me they heard the voice of a loved one who recently died. These mystical experiences had a positive effect on the man. He was more mature than others in his age group, and he developed a quiet self-confidence.

This young man's comment about putting himself in a zone also shows a remarkable insight. Wise people, going back to Patanjali, a Hindu sage 2200 years ago, have said that psychic experiences are much more frequent if we first quiet the mind. Modern figures such as José Silva and the psychologist Charles Tart have also emphasized this point. They advise going to Alpha, a state of relaxed attention with characteristic brain waves, to have psychic experiences.

The inmate's encounter with deceased family members is not unusual, although more of the stories I hear about spirits of family members involve cousins. For reasons not fully understood, there has been an alarming increase in asthma in the inner cities. I have heard several stories of a cousin dying in a man's arms while they were waiting for an ambulance during an asthma attack. Later, these men often report encounters with the deceased cousin, most frequently in their dreams, but sometime in a state of quiet relaxation.

MYSTICAL EXPERIENCES

Often an encounter with a ghost is comforting rather than frightening. The following two stories are from suburban folks. The first is from Ed, a man in his early fifties and of Native American descent on his mother's side.

Fragrance

When we were small kids, my mother used to take me and my sister with her when she went into the city shopping. She'd always stop at the perfume counter in the department store and use all the samples. We'd say, "No, Mom. Just use one. It doesn't smell good when you mix them all together." She'd say, "No. I'm doing this for a reason. I want you to remember this."

Ed's eyes watered as he said, "She's been dead for years, but every once in a while I still get that smell. That's when I know she's here."

Mary, a woman in her early sixties, told a story similar to Ed's. Her late husband was a heavy smoker and had died two years earlier.

Smoke

I moved to a new place, smaller, after Jim died. I didn't need all that space anymore. I don't smoke, and it's a new place, no prior owners, but sometimes I smell cigarette smoke. When I get that smell, it feels like Jim is there with me, and that feels good.

These experiences had a positive effect on both people. They felt certain that they would survive the death of their physical body. They no longer feared death and thought it would bring reunion with loved ones. At the same time, they respected life and were not eager to die.

Often encounters with ghosts are not frightening, and sometimes people do not even realize they've met a ghost until later. The next two stories were told by young African-American men from Baltimore.

Jack Farrell

Uncle Townie

My Uncle Townie lived with us, but he got sick and they took him to the hospital. One day my mother and father got a phone call and they went to see him. About four o'clock my Uncle Townie came home an' passed me in the hall. He said, "I'm real tired. I'm goin' up to bed." Then he went upstairs.

Later, my mother and father came home, and my mother's eyes showed she had been crying. She told me, "Your uncle died this afternoon."

Mary Jane

I was friends with Mary Jane. She went past my house on the way to school and I'd walk with her. We walked home together too. I never took her out, but sometimes she'd tell me things. Once she said, "Nicole likes you. You should ask her out."

One day I waited a long time for her, but she didn't show and I was late for school. I saw her on the way home, and she looked upset. We talked for a minute, then she said, "Freddie, I gotta go," and she was gone.

When I got home my mother said, "I'm sorry, Freddie, I have bad news. Your friend Mary Jane's house burned down last night. They all died in the fire."

When these two young men related their stories, they felt puzzled and were still processing the implications. On the cognitive level they realized they had encountered ghosts, but they had not yet made emotional changes.

Most often, mystical experiences produce profound emotional changes. Sometimes, however, there is no change, or it is relatively minor. That was the case with Karl, a ski instructor. Karl's family had emigrated to the U.S. from Switzerland when he was a child. He told this story:

MYSTICAL EXPERIENCES

Uncle Willy

Before they came to the U.S. there was an extended family gathering at a mountain chalet to celebrate New Year's Eve. Willy, Karl's favorite uncle, had gone mountain climbing with friends, but was expected back before dinner. When Willy did not show up on time, the family discussed whether they should wait for Willy or go ahead and eat. Karl remembered the incident only dimly, but he was reminded of it by relatives several times over the years. He was only five at the time, and he insisted, "No. Uncle Willy is here. He's here."

A half hour later the family received a phone call. Willy was tethered to another climber who went first. At a dangerous place the companion went ahead before Willy had time to anchor with a piton, and the companion fell. They were linked by a rope, and the man pulled Willy with him. Both men fell to their death.

Karl sensed the presence of his uncle after the man died, but this did not produce the changes I see in others who had mystical experiences. Karl is now an agnostic and only believes in the material world. Perhaps the event took place too early in his life. His story does, though, illustrate the greater sensitivity of children to the presence of spirits. Many children feel the presence of spirits, and some child therapists believe that often the imaginary playmates of children are actually spirits of deceased children. Unfortunately, this ability to relate to spirits gets discouraged by adults, and children lose their ability to connect with spirits as they grow up.

There are several books describing visitations by ghosts and other mystical experiences, but they tend to neglect the emotional and maturational changes these experiences produce. Some say that those who see spirits of the dead are crazy or flaky, but this is not the case. The great majority of mystical experiences produce an increase in emotional maturity, more confidence, and a decreased fear of death. It is not only inmates and psychotherapy patients who report encounters with spirits. Many of those who have had experiences with spirits have been among the most healthy and productive members of society.

Sir Arthur Conan Doyle, author of the Sherlock Holmes books; Lewis Carroll, author of *Alice's Adventures in Wonderland*; and the British Prime Minister William Gladstone are just a few who reported these phenomena. One of the more interesting examples was Canadian prime minister William L. Mackenzie King, who lived from 1874 to 1950. Mackenzie King was a brilliant leader who served non-consecutive terms as prime minister totaling 22 years. Apart from his government service, Mackenzie King contributed greatly to the Allied victory in World War II. The Allied leaders, including Churchill, Stalin and DeGaulle, all had massive egos. Nor was Franklin D. Roosevelt a shrinking violet. These men had difficulty cooperating, agreeing on plans, and working together. Conceding to another's view went against the grain for all four of them. Mackenzie King played a key role in reconciling differences and helping the Allied leaders reach consensus. With characteristic modesty he summed up his contributions to Canada and to the Allied effort by saying, "I really believe that my greatest service is the many unwise steps I prevent."

Mackenzie King consulted spirits on a frequent basis, especially his deceased parents, his best friend and also his political mentor. Some of this was known during his lifetime, but he had to remain discreet about it. After his death, his diaries revealed the full extent of his contact with spirits. He felt that his summer home, in a beautiful area across the Rideau River from the capital, Ottawa, was a particularly good place for contacting his deceased mother. He bequeathed the home and huge estate to the people of Canada, where it is now called Gatineau Provincial Park.

It is a peaceful place, and in the house his favorite chair, large and comfortable, rested near the fireplace. In that part of Canada, a fire is needed on the chilly nights of even late summer. The setting is ideal for Alpha, the relaxed waking state conducive to psychic experiences. When Mackenzie King thought about retiring in 1948, he consulted the spirit of FDR for advice. Roosevelt told him that it was the right time to retire, and Mackenzie King did so. This was three years after FDR's death in April of 1945.

Since the belief in spirits is found in every culture, and so many people report encounters with spirits, I have concluded that there is more to the world than matter and material. Interestingly, many devout people, regardless of their particular religious path, believe that humans are not a physical body that contains a soul or spirit. Instead they believe that we are primarily spiritual beings who have taken on a physical body.

This chapter has shown that spirits can be friendly or even helpful. They are not necessarily mischievous or frightening. Of course, they are a problem at times, and then we need a way to deal with them. That is the topic of the next chapter.

Chapter Three

Dealing with Ghosts and Possession

Spirits can trouble the living to a point that an expert must be brought in to deal with them. Some spiritual entities are not benevolent. Many who have seen the movie *The Exorcist* are not aware that it was adapted from a true story. Dangers can be involved. In this chapter the spirits are not malevolent; they are simply people who became stuck on the Earth plane after their death. This can happen for various reasons: they may not realize they have died, they may need forgiveness, they may have an emotional issue such as jealousy, or they may feel a false sense that they are needed.

The following story concerns a person who wanted forgiveness for things done in life. The story comes from Annette, a counselor at a Christian church in the Midwest.

Annette's Story

Melanie, a parishioner at the church, came to Annette because Melanie had been having disturbing dreams in which her long deceased father-in-law appeared. Melanie, who was now in her sixties, was taking care of her sick husband, Albert, who had a terminal illness. Melanie disclosed that in life her father-in-law was a harsh man. He was tough on his son, Albert, and before Albert married Melanie, he was unpleasant and occasionally rude to her.

Annette, the counselor, suggested that Melanie's father-in-law might be appearing because he needed forgiveness. With counseling Melanie was able to forgive her deceased father-in-law. She reported to Annette that after she forgave her father-in-law, he stopped appearing in her dreams.

Forgiveness is a frequent theme in the stories I hear. There seems to be good reason why the major religions emphasize forgiveness. There are also other factors in dreams or encounters with spirits of the deceased.

In September 2008 I talked with Mrs. D.G. House, an outstanding artist of Cherokee descent, when she was artist in residence at the Colter Bay Center in Grand Teton National Park. Her paintings evince a quiet sense of dignity, particularly in the way she depicts animals. As we talked, I noticed a newspaper on a nearby table opened to an article about the TV show *Ghost Hunters*. I asked Mrs. House if she had seen the series and what she thought of it. She said that she thought the show performed a valuable service by making people more aware of spirits, but she was disappointed that "once they find one, they don't do anything to help the ghost."

Mrs. House has a valid point. Most of the people who have studied ghosts and hauntings believe that ghosts are souls who got lost or stuck in the Earth plane after the death of their physical bodies. The Nobel prize-winning poet William Butler Yeats made an extensive study of the topic. He went to many séances. Yeats said that ghosts often are not aware that they have died. The spirit needs to move on but does not know it, or does not know where to go.

Linda, a woman in her mid sixties, related a story further illustrating how the dead can trouble the living. Linda's younger sister Mary Ann had died of breast cancer a few years before, and Linda's mother, Anita, had recently died in her mid eighties. When Linda herself was recovering from surgery, her mother Anita made a visitation and talked late into the night. This continued several nights in a row and caused Linda to lose sleep. It interfered with Linda's recovery from surgery. Finally one night an exasperated Linda said,

MYSTICAL EXPERIENCES

"Mom, you have to stop coming to me so late. I need my sleep. You are dead."

Her mother insisted, "I am not."

Mary Ann came into the picture and said, "Yes Mom, it's true. We're dead."

At that point the mother stopped lengthy visitations late at night and made only a few brief additional ones at more convenient times. I know Linda well enough to know she was not hallucinating and that she handled a difficult situation as best she could.

Other cultures have developed ways to handle such problems. About twenty-five years ago I attended a talk by Twylah Nitsch, a wise woman from the Wolf Clan Teaching Lodge of the Seneca people in western New York State. She taught the traditional prayer of her people for dealing with a ghost:

Traditional Mohawk and Seneca Prayer to Free an Earth Bound Spirit

Oh great and eternal Spirit,
My presence is in your presence.
My lack and limitations are now set aside,
All barriers are down and channels are clear.
I am under the protection of the four winds,
Under the direction of the Infinite Spirit,
I reach out and touch the earth bound spirit.
The rainbow of peace surrounds us.
We become the same spirit substance.
Through the power of faith,
We lift through the power of peace to the light of love.
The earth bound spirit is free to grow in peace and contentment.
Both of us are uplifted.
We are both released and uplifted
And we thank all our ancestors and relatives.

It has been said.
We thank you Great Spirit.

—Twylah Nitsch

I have used this prayer on only one occasion. To build a prison where I later worked, the state had acquired a large tract of land in central Maryland. There were houses on the property, a few small bungalows and one large Victorian-style mansion. These buildings were outside the fenced perimeter of the prison, and the smaller houses were used as homes by higher-ranking officials. There were attempts to use the larger building, but many people refused to go in after seeing a ghost. Although stories of ghosts usually place them at night, most of the sightings of this ghost occurred during the daylight hours.

Even the commander of the guards, a tough hombre who rode a Harley, refused to go in again after seeing the ghost. I did not see the ghost myself, but I tend to hear them or feel their presence rather than see them. I went to the building and said the Mohawk-Seneca prayer I had learned from Twylah Nitsch. No one reported seeing the ghost after I did that.

I am not sure if I can take any credit for the ghost's leaving. It may have been coincidental. Many other things changed at about the same time. A new governor was elected, and he appointed new officials. Several employees, including the commander of the guards, moved on to other jobs. The newcomers had not heard the story about the ghost, and there were no incidents. The state now uses the building as a personnel office without problems.

Although Christian, I respect the Native American prayer for dealing with ghosts. It feels more gentle than some of the Christian prayers for de-possession, which tend to command rather than persuade the spirit to leave. It is important to note that both the Christian and the Native American approaches contain prayer elements for protection of the person doing the intervention. In both traditions it is believed that without a prayer for protection, the ghost can possess the person doing the intervention.

Charlie, a middle-aged private practice patient, told me of another example where a spirit possessed a house. He had been divorced a few years when he met a widow, Natalie. They began dating and eventually married. He moved in with Natalie because her home was close to her work, while his would have been too long a commute for her. In her home Charlie felt like someone else was present, and he often heard strange noises at night. Charlie consulted Tracy, a psychic with a good reputation for dealing with spirits. Tracy asked how Tim, Natalie's former husband, had died. Charlie told her it was by suicide. Tracy asked if a pet was killed and if there was water nearby.

There was a pool in the backyard, and shortly before his suicide Tim had taken the family dog for a walk along a highway without a leash. The dog was killed. Tracy told Charlie that Tim had planned to commit suicide for a long time but did not want to cross over alone. Natalie had been in danger. Tim considered killing her first, but decided on the dog instead. Tracy also said Tim was jealous of Charlie and that was one of the reasons he continued to stay at the home. Tracy came from another part of the state, and it was unlikely she could have learned the details by other means. These comments convinced Charlie that Tracy had a gift, and he asked her to come to the home and do a clearing.

Tracy came to the home with a supply of sage incense sticks. Although it was twenty-five years after Tim's death, Tracy was able to contact his spirit. She told him that his presence was harming both the living and himself. It was harming him because he needed to move toward the light to get on with the next stage of his development. She repeated this several times and went through the house burning the sage incense, making gestures toward the windows with them. Next Tracy made cross signs with the incense at each window and door. Charlie felt that the clearing worked. He no longer feels a presence and said that the atmosphere in the house feels much lighter.

Dr. Carl A. Wickland, a Swedish-born American psychiatrist, believed that spirit possession was a factor in some mental illnesses, particularly in opium and morphine addiction. These addictions were a serious social problem in the U.S. in the late 1800s and early 1900s. Before the Food and Drug Administration was established to control these drugs, they could be obtained over the counter from pharmacies with relative ease. Addiction to opium and related drugs hit housewives especially hard. The playwright Eugene O'Neill portrayed this problem vividly in his masterpiece *Long Day's Journey into Night*.

With the collaboration of his wife, Wickland set up a small clinic in Los Angeles in 1918 and took in a small number of patients at a time, usually six to ten, and treated them until they were in good health. Wickland believed that when some alcoholics or drug addicted people die, their spirit continues to crave the substance they abused during life. Often they do not even realize that they have died. Their spirit then possesses a person to try to vicariously satisfy their craving. Wickland presented a number of case histories in which he made de-possession a part of the treatment process. He produced good results, and often both the spirit and the possessed, addicted patient thanked Dr. Wickland at the end of treatment.

Dr. Edith Fiore, a psychologist who practiced in California for many years but is now retired in Florida, has written several books on the topic. Like Dr. Wickland, Dr. Fiore believes that spirit possession is a factor in a number of psychological problems, especially addictions, whether to alcohol, drugs, food, cigarettes, or sex. She believes that spirits who were addicted to something during their lifetimes will often try to possess a living person to continue to experience their desire after death.

MYSTICAL EXPERIENCES

When she believes it is appropriate, Dr. Fiore incorporates de-possession into her psychological treatment. Her approach is similar to the Seneca in that it is also gentle. She considers the possessing spirit to be another one of her patients. She explains to him or her that his body is dead, and that his presence is harming both himself and the person who is possessed. Sometimes she holds a mirror up to the possessed person and tells him to look at the reflection and see that he is not in his own body. She also assures him that he will be better off when he is at his correct place. Finally, she bids him to go in peace with her blessings.

Although many mainstream psychologists do not agree with her theories, Dr. Fiore's results are impressive. She believes that three places are danger zones for spirit possession: bars, hospitals, and cemeteries. Bars are dangerous because spirits who were alcoholic during life seek to re-experience alcohol. In addition, alcohol weakens our auras, our major defense against possession. Hospitals are dangerous because people often die there while they are unconscious or confused, and their spirit may seek another body. Cemeteries are also places where numbers of spirits are present. Whether we agree with Dr. Fiore or not, many of her readers feel it is prudent to say a silent prayer for protection before entering bars, hospitals or cemeteries.

Both Dr. Fiore and David St. Clair, who studied spirit possession in Brazil, recommend an exercise in addition to prayer if anyone attempts a de-possession. They recommend that when attempting de-possession, one should visualize a protective white light surrounding him, similar to the protective force fields around spaceships in science fiction movies. The exercise of visualizing white light around oneself for protection may seem trivial to some, but it has been recommended by psychics from widely disparate cultures.

In addition to the white light exercise, Dr. Fiore recommends keeping one's aura strong, since people are more easily possessed if their auras are weak. To test your aura, put your hands in the prayer position but not quite touching. After you feel some energy between your palms (it may feel like heat or static electricity), slowly move the palms apart. If you lose the feeling of energy, move them closer until you feel it again. The point is to get them as far apart as possible as long as you still feel energy. Various teachers say that alcohol or drug abuse weakens auras. To strengthen the aura, spiritual teachers recommend outdoor exercise such as walking while breathing deeply. Many say the practice of Tai Chi, and also Qi Gong, strengthens the aura.

I have witnessed only one de-possession. A young woman was severely depressed, in the depressed phase of bipolar disorder. She was not my patient, but I was one of three mental health professionals present. The de-possession was done by a Brazilian *spiritista* accompanied by the patient's therapist. After the spirits were told they were in a body that did not belong to them, suddenly voices came, not from the patient, but from the mouth of a woman psychiatrist who was present. There were two different voices; one was female and the other an older male. The male voice said, "No, I don't want to go." Both voices had accents totally different from the psychiatrist's. It took some convincing, but the spirits were finally persuaded to leave. I later learned from the patient's therapist that the de-possession helped with the episode of severe depression, but did not cure the bipolar illness.

At our present stage of civilization we tend to think of ourselves as more advanced than the peoples of earlier eras. While this is certainly true in regard to our technology, it is not true in all areas. Some wisdom has been lost along the way. One area of lost wisdom involves the shamans of the past. Dr. Mircea Eliade, a Romanian-born scholar who taught at the University of Chicago for many years, has written about the role of shamans as "psychopomps," or the guide of souls.

MYSTICAL EXPERIENCES

In ancient times when a person in the village was dying, the shaman of the village made a trance journey, and as the dying person's spirit left the body, the shaman guided the spirit to the correct place in the lower world. This was usually the place where loved ones, friends, and relatives who had previously died were located. Then the person who had just died was reunited with family and friends. Having guided the friends and relatives on previous journeys, the shaman knew where to bring the spirit that had just left the body.

Many believe that shamans used hallucinogenic plants to make trance journeys, but scholars have found that less than fifteen percent of shamanic cultures used hallucinogens. Dr. Michael Harner has shown that most used the monotonous beat of a drum at a particular frequency to make a trance journey. Early explorers such as Knud Rasmussen and Peter Freuchen described powerful shamans among the indigenous peoples of Arctic Canada and Greenland. These peoples had few plants, and certainly not hallucinogenic ones.

Peter Freuchen described shamanic knowledge of the death of two people with absolutely no hallucinogens. Knud Rasmussen had left Thule several months earlier as part of the second expedition across the Greenland ice cap. An expedition across Greenland was a formidable undertaking in the early 1900s; the interior was unexplored territory. At that time there was no GPS for navigation, no radios to call for assistance, no air support to bring emergency supplies.

Freuchen had remained at their base in Thule on the west coast of Greenland, and he reported that on one evening a group of local people had gathered in the building where he lived. An older woman, Inaluk, suddenly jumped up and went outside without her coat. A few minutes later they heard her singing and went out. She was swaying in the moonlight, her long black hair switching across her face as she sang: "Those who have been to the east side are back. Those who have been to the east side are back."

When she came out of the trance Freuchen asked if everyone had made it, and Inaluk told him that two people were missing. Freuchen asked if Rasmussen was missing, but Inaluk was derisive about that question. She said that the ice cap could not get the better of Knud. She told Freuchen that two others did not make it.

Several hours later the guests had gone home, but Freuchen was unable to sleep. During the night the haggard Rasmussen stuck his head through the door. Freuchen was overjoyed to see his friend, but he noticed that months of hardship and starvation showed on Knud's face. Freuchen asked if everyone had made it. Rasmussen reported that they had lost two people: Henrik Olsen had been devoured by wolves, and Dr. Wulff had to be left behind to die.

In my view, a natural trance such as Inaluk's is better than one achieved with hallucinogens because the thinking is clear. When trance is achieved through drugs, thinking can be muddled. Chanting or a continuous drum beat at a particular frequency are good ways of achieving trance, but some experienced people like Inaluk can do it without any procedure.

There are many other stories of shaman clairvoyance among the indigenous Arctic people in Freuchen and Rasmussen's accounts of their explorations. Rasmussen told the story of Quillarsuaq, a particularly powerful shaman from Baffin Island in Canada. He was so powerful that at night he had a nimbus of white light shining around his head similar to that in portraits of early Christian saints.

In 1856 Quillarsauq told a group from his village that there were people far to the north who had little food and were living in semi-starvation. Quillarsuaq assembled a rescue party that traveled 500 miles on foot across mountains, rivers and straits between islands. Finally in 1863 they found an Inuit group near Siorapaluk in

MYSTICAL EXPERIENCES

Greenland. Those people lived in a constant state of insufficient food. They had lost many survival skills, such as building kayaks and hunting with a bow and arrow.

The Baffin Islanders stayed with them for five years, teaching better fishing skills, building kayaks for hunting seals, and making bows and arrows for hunting caribou. Eventually the Baffin Islanders started for the trip home. Quillarsuaq had led them to Greenland through his clairvoyant powers, but he died on the trip home. The others did not know the way, and they had no choice. They returned to Siorapaluk and settled among the people they had come to assist.

To summarize Section One, ghost stories and encounters with spirits serve to show that the soul or spirit lives on after the death of the physical body. Reports of encounters with spirits of the deceased are widespread and exist in all cultures. The socioeconomic level of the people makes no difference. Some of the inmates who made reports came from impoverished backgrounds, while some of the patients in my private practice were affluent.

Nor does education make a difference. Some of the inmates I work with dropped out in the early grades. On the other hand, Mackenzie King, the Canadian Prime Minister, had a B.A. and a law degree from a Canadian university, plus a Ph.D. in economics from Harvard.

Consulting the spirits of the deceased was much more popular in the late 1800s and early 1900s, but after frauds were detected, interest dropped. Logically, this makes as much sense as concluding real money does not exist because of a few encounters with counterfeit money. There are enough reports of spirits or ghosts from credible people to warrant consideration that the soul or spirit may survive the death of the physical body.

Some psychics recommend caution in using the Ouija board or other techniques for contacting spirits. They say that not all spirits are benevolent, and lower entities may be attracted. It is also a good idea to have a person with some experience do a de-possession or clear a house. There is a reason most cultures include a prayer for protection before attempting to contact spirits. It is wise to use both a prayer from your own religious tradition and the technique recommended by David St. Clair of visualizing yourself surrounded by a protective light. These protective measures are important, because we can be possessed by a spirit who has goals that are against our best interests. Dr. Edith Fiore has found that some of her patients with addictions had become possessed by spirits who wanted to re-experience alcohol, drugs or an addictive behavior.

Part II

Protection by a Higher Power

Chapter Four

A Higher Power Often Protects Us

Many religions believe that there is a God, gods, or a Higher Power in the universe that helps and protects us more often than we realize. A large number of patients from both ends of the economic spectrum have told me stories relating protection by a Higher Power. The following six stories were selected from the many I have heard over the years.

Of course, we are not protected all the time, and bad things do happen to good people. I struggle to understand why we are protected only some of the time. That issue will be dealt with in the next chapter.

Dozens of inmates told me they received supernatural warnings. Usually the warnings were general. Many low-level drug dealers live a violent lifestyle selling drugs, using the money they make to get high and party. They must fight to defend their territory against rival gangs. Many of these young men said they were visited by ghosts of former companions who had been killed in shootouts. The ghosts often told them, "Get off the street. Get outta the drug game."

Unfortunately, most inmates who received these warnings did not heed them and continued to sell drugs. The pull is too strong. These men have a choice between a job that pays little above minimum wage versus making thousands per night selling drugs. In addition, their money and access to drugs brings an abundance of available females.

Since they do not do long-term planning, very few drug dealers keep any money after arrests. The tracking of financial transactions to prevent money laundering limits the investment opportunities of dealers. An inmate who lost everything after he got arrested told me, "I think my ex-girlfriend has my car. Some cops snatched my gun collection, and my landlord took my gold chains. When you go to jail, your shit just goes away."

Sometimes supernatural warnings are specific. This story was told to me by a nineteen-year-old African-American man incarcerated in a medium-security prison:

Get Outta the Car

I was smokin' weed with my cousin at my aunt's house. My aunt won't have marijuana in the house. We have to go out. It was a cold-ass night, so we sat in my sister's car smokin' and chillin'. Now the car is parked around the corner at the bottom of a big hill. We were smokin' awhile when I hear this voice inside my head: "Get outta the car. Get outta the car." I told my cousin, "Get outta this car." We both jumped out, and a few seconds later this big SUV comes down the hill way too fast. It swings wide around the corner and crashes into my sister's car so hard it goes on top. Crushed the whole top half of the car. Someone said he was on PCP.

The young man became visibly shaken as he recounted this story, which had happened approximately a year earlier. How was he warned? With over six billion people in the world, it seems unlikely that God personally protects all of us. It is more likely we are protected through an intermediary. Many traditions believe that we are assigned helping spirits or a guardian angel, and given the number of people on the planet, this makes sense.

The next story is from Sandra, a retired woman who retained her good looks although she was in her late sixties.

MYSTICAL EXPERIENCES

Icy Morning

We moved into our new house a few months before my husband, Luke, died. There were no other houses around here at that time. I had been talking to my son, Billy. He was working the night shift, and he said that he'd visit me about noon the next day. He wanted to get a little sleep before he came over.

I got up early the next day and went out to get the paper at about six-twenty. We had had an ice storm during the night, and it was slippery. I slipped and fell down the steps. I broke my leg and couldn't get up. It was real cold, and I was only wearing a light robe over my pajamas. There were no neighbors, so yelling wouldn't help. I thought Billy would get here too late to save me and I was going to freeze to death. I said some prayers while I waited to die. Then I heard Billy as he came to me. He said something told him to come straight here, don't go home for sleep after work.

Of course, it may have been chance that Billy decided to visit his mother earlier than planned, but Sandra is convinced that she had spiritual help that prompted him. I have heard so many similar stories that I am convinced that much of the time we actually get help.

The following story is from Jackson, who lives in central Maryland near Washington, D.C. In Maryland there are places where soil conditions occasionally cause sinkholes to appear, often in less than convenient locations.

Difficult Commute

I was driving to work on the D.C. beltway, and a big van blocked my view of the road ahead. Suddenly the van swerved. Then I saw this deep sinkhole wider than my car right in front of me. It was too late for me to swerve, and traffic was heavy. I thought, *I'll go into the hole and the cars behind will crash into me.* I thought I was going to die and said a quick prayer: "God, please help me."

I went into the hole, and I had a funny feeling that time slowed down, that everything was happening in slow motion. My car bounced and it felt like it was lifted up. It seems impossible, but the front wheels grabbed the road at the top of the hole and I was able to keep going. There's not many people I say this to, but I think angels lifted my car.

A similar incident in different circumstances happened to a young nurse. Terri's hobby was photography, and she and her husband were driving through the southwestern U.S. She spotted an interesting desert vista with a dramatic cloud formation in the background, and she asked her husband to stop. She moved around the area to find the best angle for photos. After taking a couple of shots, Terri felt a strike on the back of her right calf. She was engrossed in picture taking and hardly noticed until she felt two more strikes.

Looking down, she saw she was standing on a western diamondback. Her foot was on the head and neck of the snake, so it must have hit her with its body. She was terrified to move, because stepping off the snake would make her vulnerable to the fangs. She yelled for her husband and he started running, but he was a good distance away. Suddenly Terri felt hands beneath her shoulders lift her up and set her down about thirty feet away. Terri told me about this four years after it happened, but both fear and astonishment showed on her face as she told the story.

Numerous patients have reported getting help in the form of strange coincidences. Jim was a young scholar who had recently obtained his Ph.D. and was making a good salary for the first time. He was fond of art and used his new affluence to buy a large watercolor painting. He had it framed under glass and hung it on the wall behind the bed in his apartment. This is what he told me:

MYSTICAL EXPERIENCES

Watercolor

About a quarter to twelve on a Friday night I got a call from Jeannie, my friend downstairs. She said she had gotten two phone calls. They didn't say anything, but she heard heavy breathing and then hang-ups. She was scared and asked me if I would come down for a while. I had never gone out with Jeannie, but we hung out with the same group and were buddies. I went downstairs. Jeannie fixed some decaf and we talked for about an hour. Then Jeannie felt reassured, and I went back to my own place. When I went into my bedroom, I was shocked. My painting had fallen off the wall, and there was shattered glass all over my pillow. I could have been hurt or killed.

Of course, Jim's experience could have been a coincidence, but I have heard too many stories of people being saved by a coincidence. I believe that most things are caused rather than coincidental. The next story involves a coincidence, but perhaps not a mere coincidence. I learned this story through Betsy's mother.

Betsy's Story

Betsy, a Maryland resident, was a student at the University of Virginia in Charlottesville, about three hours from her home. She spent a weekend with her parents, and when she went to drive back to the university on Sunday evening, her Volkswagen would not start. Her father, who is good with cars, could not start it either. Finally her parents said, "It's getting late. Why don't you take our Mercedes back to school, and we'll take care of your car tomorrow."

Betsy took her parents' car, but going through a hilly section she hit a patch of black ice. The car went over the side and rolled over several times as it plunged down a hill. She was wearing her seat belt, and thanks to the sturdy Mercedes, Betsy was only bruised and shaken up. If she had been in the Volkswagen, there might have been a different outcome. The strangest part is that when

Betsy's parents got the call next morning and went down to see her, the Volkswagen started up with no problem.

I believe that this is one of many examples of a Higher Power helping us. Often we are helped through an intermediary, perhaps an angel or a spirit. The next story is from Mitch, a retired teacher and an avid hunter.

Deer Season

It was the second day of deer season. Early in the morning I was at one of my favorite spots, partway down a hillside over a narrow valley. On the way in I saw three guys on the opposite slope, but I didn't think anything of it. I was waiting when I saw a beautiful five-point buck just a little down the hill from me. As I was taking aim, a big owl flew up, almost hitting me in the face. It made me step back and to the side. No sooner had I moved than bullets slammed into the hillside where I had been. Those guys on the opposite slope fired without looking at what was past the buck. Owls don't fly in the daytime, but that one did. He saved my life.

Owls usually avoid people and do not fly into faces. As Mitch noted, they are nocturnal and are rarely seen during the day. This raises questions: Did an angel or spiritual intermediary take on the form of an owl? Do animals perform spiritual tasks more often than we know?

People can have a hunch that turns out to be correct, but I have wondered, where do hunches come from? Do we get spiritual prompting when a hunch springs into mind? Consider the case of Ben and his wife Lucy. Lucy went through a period of depression, but she was in denial that she had a problem. Occasionally depression manifests as anger, and it did so with Lucy. She blamed Ben for the terrible way she felt, asked for a divorce, and insisted he move out. Ben moved out and got his own apartment. There were times when he had to meet Lucy to discuss finances, taxes, or the

MYSTICAL EXPERIENCES

children's education. On these occasions Lucy often became seductive and they would have sex. Ben found this confusing.

Late one night Ben got a call from Lucy. She said that she wanted to end it all, and she had taken an overdose of sedatives. On the phone she sounded sleepy, and at times her voice would fade. Lucy complained that she wanted to sleep, but trucks kept starting up and would wake her. Then the phone went dead.

Lucy lived near the intersection of two major interstate highways, and the area has several motels, gas stations and restaurants that welcome truckers. There were more than a dozen possibilities, but the thought of a rest stop about ten miles away on one of the highways sprang into Ben's mind. He drove there as fast as he dared and found Lucy's car, but she had lost consciousness. He was able to get her to an emergency room, and they saved her. The doctors told Ben he got her in just in time. Any later and she would not have made it.

She was held in the mental health unit for a week. The doctors convinced Lucy of the need for treatment for her depression, and marital counseling for both of them. She continued treatment with a combination of anti-depression medication and psychotherapy. This has been successful, and they are reunited.

Of the many possibilities, why did Ben choose that particular rest stop? It seems impossible that pure chance was at work. I believe it is much more likely that Ben received a prompt from a spiritual source.

Sonia, a Peruvian woman who works as a tour guide for a travel company, told me of two dramatic examples when she believes that she received help from spiritual sources. On the "Ring of Fire," Peru experiences frequent earthquakes. Sonia had a room on the ninth floor of a high-rise hotel in Lima, while three single tourists had rooms on the same floor. Couples in her group had rooms on lower floors.

During the night Sonia was awakened by the violent shaking of an earthquake. She ran out of the room in her nightclothes, fearful that the building might collapse, but she also feared going out into the street, where she might be injured by falling debris. In the hallway a man in white clothing told her not to leave. The three tourists also came into the hall, where the man told the four of them to hold hands with him in a circle and pray.

She said that the man led the prayers in English, saying, "Pray with us. We are brothers and sisters. My father loves you and protects you. My father is with us." He continued the prayers throughout the earthquake. The next morning Sonia asked the hotel manager who was the fifth guest on the ninth floor. The manager replied there was no fifth guest, only herself and three tourists on that floor.

Sonia got another surprise when she questioned the three tourists who had joined her in prayer with the man in white. When they described him, one said he was a policeman, and another said he looked like a backpacker and had a long ponytail. Sonia was puzzled by the different perceptions of the man and wondered whether the man in white could have been an angel.

In another incident Sonia was about to take a group of fifteen tourists from Lima across the Andes to Iquitos, a small city in the Amazon rainforest of northeastern Peru. At the Lima airport their flight was delayed several times because of bad weather on the route to Iquitos. Finally their flight and all other flights to Iquitos that day were canceled.

The next day the airline presented Sonia with a difficult decision. There would be a flight to Iquitos, but only eight seats were available. Sonia wondered if she should split her group and send some on ahead, hoping to join them later, or wait until they could all go together. As she considered this, Sonia heard a voice in her head: "Do not go. Do not get on that plane." Sonia decided to wait another day until a plane could take her entire group. The plane with only eight available seats crashed, killing most passengers. Sonia believes the voice in her head had a spiritual source.

There are many scholars who have written about spiritual helpers. Rabbi David Cooper has written knowledgably about angels. Carolyn Myss has said that we get a great deal of help from spirits all the time, but that we are unaware of it. She believes we get help even with mundane tasks like crossing the street.

The former Harvard psychologist Richard Alpert changed his name to Baba Ram Dass after studying with Maharaji, an enlightened man in India. Ram Dass has said that there are spirits all around us just waiting to help, but they prefer to be asked. Most of the material I have read agrees with this point—the spirit helpers want to be asked, and they like to be thanked afterward.

A patient who came to the U.S. from Southeast Asia told me that he often asks for help from spirits and gets it, even with unexceptional matters. He said that if he cannot find his keys when he has to leave for work in the morning, he will say, "Spirits, please help me find my keys." The patient said after doing that, most of the time he receives a mental image of a particular place. When he checks that place, it is usually where he finds his keys. He said that he thanks the spirits afterward, which seems to ensure he gets help the next time.

In Colorado I saw an amusing variation of this practice when the snow was not deep enough for good skiing. Some skiers poured the liqueur Jaegermeister on the snow in the evening as an offering to the mountain spirits, asking them to bring in good snow overnight. I have no idea whether or not this worked, nor how much Jaegermeister was consumed beforehand.

Chapter Five

Why Do We Get Help Only Some of the Time?

My friend Naomi survived the Holocaust as a child, and she is an atheist. When I told her about the material in the previous chapter, she challenged me, asking, "Where was God at Auschwitz?" I had no answer for her. Naomi is not alone in grappling with this issue. Both non-fiction works on spirituality and novels with a spiritual theme question whether God exists, or take God to task for the evil in the world.

The stories I have heard convince me that we often get help from God, usually through intermediaries such as angels or helping spirits. Yet we often do not get what we pray for, and bad things, even terrible things, happen to good people. It is easier to deal with not getting what we pray for. The following story came from Richard, a scientist.

Lab Assistant

When I was a grad student, I had a tough time financially. I had gotten married early, and my wife was a high school teacher. We figured that with her salary plus the stipend I got from the university, we'd be O.K., but she got pregnant and had to quit teaching. Finances got tight, and we were just scraping by.

Then I saw an ad for a great job, a lab assistant at an institute where they were studying the biological effects of radiation. This was when the Cold War was on, and everyone was scared about atomic war and radiation. The salary was good, benefits were great, and the work hours were a good fit with my class schedule. The job involved taking care of the lab animals, which I knew I would like. I wasn't crazy about exposing them to radiation, but I figured it was for a good cause and I was willing.

I applied for the job and prayed hard to get it. The choice narrowed down to me and one other guy, George. Finally they selected him. I figured my prayers were not answered, and I muddled through the financial problems with a combination of student loans, an assistantship and occasional jobs until I got my Ph.D.

About five or six years later I was working at a research institute when George came on board as another scientist. We didn't become close friends, but we got along O.K. After he was there a bit over a year, George started taking off a lot of time, mostly sick leave. We saw less and less of him, and then after a longer absence, George died of lung cancer. He had never smoked, and he was a young man in his early thirties. I've often wondered if occupational exposure to radiation at that lab caused it. And I wonder if God was taking good care of me by not giving me the job I prayed for.

Explaining the presence of suffering in the world is far more difficult than dealing with unanswered prayers. Many people, including major scholars such as Leibnitz and Spinoza, have struggled with this issue without reaching consensus. Rabbi Harold Kushner struggled with the same after his son died of progeria, a rare and terrible disease where the body ages prematurely. Children with this condition develop wrinkled skin, gray hair and the facial appearance and mannerisms of old age.

His emotional pain motivated Kushner to write *When Bad Things Happen to Good People*, published in 1983. He believed that that if God were both benevolent and omnipotent, such suffering would not occur. Kushner could not believe God is not benevolent; therefore, Kushner concluded that God is not omnipotent and does not have the power to stop suffering. He felt this was especially true in a case like his son's, where God would not be violating free will if he intervened. Kushner's book became a bestseller, and for many readers it brought resolution. Other readers did not get consolation from Kushner's book.

Those who believe God not only created the world, but also sustains creation, are convinced that God does have the power to stop suffering. They believe that, for reasons unknown to us, God chooses not to intervene. The violation of free will is one possibility.

To get a view from another culture, I asked a Native American medicine man for his perspective. He told me that some suffering is required to redeem this precious life we are given. This explains the suffering in some of their rituals; for example, the Lakota Sioux Vision Quest and the Sun Dance. I could not handle these rituals on their path, but I have great respect for those who voluntarily go through them. When I asked the medicine man why some are chosen to suffer and not others, he said that it was an honor to be chosen. Those who suffer redeem not only their own lives, but also the lives of others.

A possible explanation for suffering has been put forth by those who believe in reincarnation. Baba Ram Dass, a.k.a. Dr. Richard Alpert, has said that we choose each lifetime before we jump into it. The choice is based on what we need to accomplish to reach our eventual goal, union with God. At first this might seem absurd, especially so if we go back to Naomi's question, "Where was God at Auschwitz?" This view suggests that the prisoners at Auschwitz, and the other victims of the Holocaust, volunteered for their fate before they went into that lifetime.

Why would those victims do such a thing? It may be that their suffering led to the destruction of the Nazi regime. Obviously, torture, cruelty and the killing of people destroys the victims, but it is also destructive to the perpetrators. Throughout the ages, mystics have said that cruelty coarsens people and destroys their intuitive abilities. Franz Fannon, an Algerian psychiatrist, treated French

Algerians who tortured their enemies during the hellish Algerian war for independence. To Fannon's surprise, he found that torturers pay a high price. He found that torturing is often more destructive to the mental health of those who do it than it is to those who receive it.

Hitler's cruelty caused him to lose the Second World War. When the Nazis invaded the Soviet Union, they were first greeted as liberators. Stalin had been incredibly cruel to his own citizens, particularly the ethnic minorities. Some historians believe that Stalin caused the deaths of 20 million Soviet citizens. As the Nazi invaders marched into the Soviet Union, tens of thousands of people from Belarus, the Baltic States, the Ukraine, and Russia itself volunteered to help the invaders overthrow Stalin.

But the Nazis had honed their cruelty on the Jews, and then applied it on people who could have been their allies. The people of the Soviet Union were treated abominably. Even babies were sacrificed, some drained dry of blood for transfusions. It did not take long for a patriotic feeling for Mother Russia to emerge. The people rallied to support their army, and eventually the Soviets drove the Nazis back to Berlin.

If the Nazis had treated the Soviet people well and welcomed them as allies, they would have beaten the Soviet army. No longer fighting a two-front war, the Nazis would have been a far more formidable foe on the western front in Europe. I do not wish to minimize the terrible suffering of the Holocaust, but the question of a benevolent God permitting it is extremely difficult, and I am raising one of many possible explanations. Admittedly these views are a stretch, but if true, the victims of the Holocaust were martyrs who helped save the world from the Nazis. Is it possible that God was at Auschwitz after all?

Part III

No One Is an Island – We Are Connected

Chapter Six

Separation Is an Illusion

We are not as separate as we believe. We are interconnected in both obvious and mysterious ways. Our thoughts and emotions have the power to affect others, even at a distance. Our ability to affect others can be used positively—for example, to promote healing. It can also be used negatively. Indeed, our thoughts alone can kill enemies. Cruelty and harming others are stupid, because the saying "What goes around, comes around" is true. Harming others through psychic powers is even worse. Using psychic or occult power to harm is incredibly costly for those who do it. It makes no sense at all from a cost-benefit perspective.

Buddhists have long maintained that separateness is an illusion. It is unfortunate that many U.S. leaders do not understand this point. Not only is cruelty abhorrent, it is stupid because it does not work. The interrogators at Guantanamo Bay and Abu Ghraib have squandered America's moral high ground. The lives of many American soldiers fighting in Europe in World War II were saved because of humane behavior by American soldiers in World War I. German soldiers had been told by uncles and grandfathers that if they got into a desperate situation, instead of fighting to the death, surrender to Americans.

Another example showing that harsh interrogation is ineffective comes from a number of high-level German officers who were captured in World War II. They were brought to Ft. Myer near Arlington Memorial Cemetery in Virginia for questioning. Several

U.S. interrogators said adversarial techniques did not work. One said he got much more information from a man by taking him to dinner at a good restaurant in Washington.

Some of the ways our emotions affect others are obvious and do not need a psychic explanation. I have conducted hundreds, perhaps thousands of group therapy sessions over the years, and I have observed a powerful effect many times. When a therapy group has been running long enough for a group feeling to emerge, and the members begin to feel empathy for each other, remarkable things happen.

If a patient in the group is experiencing anxiety but has not talked about it, the whole group gets edgy and feels anxious. Anxiety is communicated. Something even more remarkable in therapy groups takes place when a group member tells about a painful experience. If he is really experiencing the pain, the eyes of the other group members glisten slightly for a low-level tearing response. This is a nonverbal expression of empathy, and it takes place without conscious awareness. I have observed this many times, including among criminals in a maximum security setting.

There are more mysterious ways in which our thoughts and feelings affect others. What man has not stared at the rear of a shapely woman, only to have her suddenly turn and catch him in the act? Many women say they can "feel the pressure of eyes." The British scientist Rupert Sheldrake has conducted experiments proving that the majority of women can tell when they are being stared at, and his results are well beyond chance probability.

Most of my work with the incarcerated people I've seen in prisons has been men, but the following story comes from a short time when I worked with women inmates.

A Glass of Water: A Woman Inmate's Story

I've heard voices telling me to do bad things ever since I was a little girl, but I've learned that they're just in my head. Most of the time I don't pay attention, but the other night me and my cellmate,

MYSTICAL EXPERIENCES

Mary Alice, were walkin' back to our cell and we each had a glass of water. We saw Sally in the hall, and the voices came on really strong, tellin' me to throw my water on Sally. I fought them. It was hard, but I kept tellin' myself they're only in my head, and I didn't do it. Then all of a sudden, Mary Alice threw her water on Sally. That really surprised me, because Mary Alice is a goody two-shoes. I don't think Mary Alice ever did a bad thing in her life, except kill her husband.

The woman who told this story obviously suffered from auditory hallucinations, but she took her psychiatric medications as prescribed and she functioned reasonably well. The more interesting questions concern the other woman, Mary Alice, usually a model inmate. The first woman struggled against the impulse to throw her water on Sally. How was that impulse communicated to Mary Alice? What caused the usually well-behaved Mary Alice to give in to it?

While I do not know precisely how the woman's thought to throw her water on Sally was communicated to her friend, I know such things occur more often when two people breathe in sync. I suspect that as the two women walked down the long hallway together, they began to breathe in sync without realizing it. Breathing in sync has mysterious powers, and it is interesting to note that the Latin roots of the word "conspire" mean "breathe together."

When I treat patients, I use hypnosis when the situation calls for it. The hypnosis works faster and more powerfully when I breathe in sync with the patient. In doing marriage counseling, I often have a bickering couple sit facing each other. After relaxing a few moments, I tell them to silently stare into each other's eyes while they breathe in sync. This helps them stop the reflexive attack and counterattack, and they become more open to each other's point of view.

Breathing in sync may have facilitated the thought transfer, but more information is needed about the process. Researchers report that thought transfer like that described above can take place over distances. This is puzzling, because in all other known forms of energy, the strength of the signal decreases in proportion to the square of the distance. This does not seem to be the case with the energy in psychic phenomena.

Often the interconnectedness between people shows up in a dream, as the following young African-American man's story illustrates:

The Dream

There was lots of heroin in my neighborhood. Both my mother and my aunt died from overdoses, so my grandmother raised us. All the guys I knew fired drugs, and when I was sixteen some buddies got me to try it. At home the next day my grandmother made me and my two cousins strip down to our underwear. She checked us over: our arms, our armpits, the back of our legs.

I asked her, "What are you doin'?"

She said, "Lookin' for needle marks. Last night I had this dream, someone in our family was takin' stuff in a needle. I had that dream twice before, just before your mother and just before your aunt died. Those times I saw their faces in the dreams. This time I didn't, but I know it was someone in the family."

She checked us over for a long time and she didn't find my needle mark, but her dream scared me so much I never fired drugs again.

It can be debated whether psychic factors were involved, but at the very least, the emotional bond between the woman and her grandchildren precipitated her dream.

The following story is an example of a man who became aware of his deep connection to a woman, but he could not hold on to the relationship. The story was told by Jonathan, a divorced man. He had retired as an Army officer, and as a civilian he held a high-level position in the Defense Department. He had a sad and wistful tone as he told me this story.

MYSTICAL EXPERIENCES

Tantric Sex

I met her at a concert, and we really hit it off. She was smart, funny and cute as hell. She was into Eastern things and taught me about the I Ching, yoga, and meditation. Our sex was great, and once it was like nothing I've ever experienced. She had me do these yoga postures that she called Tantra, and breathing exercises just before sex. When we came, it was like we could see inside each other's minds. I could feel what she was feeling, and I could see what she was thinking. Kind of like what the Bible said: the two of us became as one. It was so good it scared me, and we never had it that good again.

We finally broke up. She dabbled in drugs, especially marijuana, and my security clearance was up for renewal. The real killer, though, was our different lifestyles. She liked to sleep until noon, but I had to give briefings to defend my programs at 8:00 a.m. sharp. With the commute and all, that meant getting up at 5:30, so I had to get to bed by 10:00. Then the night was only starting for her. We just couldn't make it work.

Jonathan's story reveals that a profound experience of the interconnectedness of people is often fleeting. It can be difficult or impossible to re-capture. Some years later many will wonder if such events really happened, or if they only dreamed it.

The purpose of this chapter has been to show that people are interconnected. The Buddhist belief that separation is an illusion has merit. The purpose of the next two chapters is to further explore our interconnectedness and to show that we have free will. We can use our interconnectedness to help others heal, or to harm and even kill them by psychic means. The choice is ours, but if we use it to harm, we have to accept the consequences.

Chapter Seven

Inter-Connections and Healing

The psychologist Stanley Krippner re-tells a Native American legend: Grandmother Spider has woven a great web that connects all people, as well as all the living and non-living things on Earth, to one other. In the Native American spiritual view we are all inter-connected. This might seem like an overdose of fantasy, but Hindu and Buddhist scholars agree and say that separation between people is an illusion. The Nobel prize-winning quantum physicist Erwin Schrodinger also agrees and has said, "The sum total of all the minds in the universe is one." I find quantum physics difficult to understand, but my patients have told me stories that illustrate this principle in a concrete way.

My patient Scott, who owned a small, specialized construction company, told me the following story. Scott traveled the world as a sub-contractor for much larger firms on projects. His firm performed a portion of the construction of a resort-hotel complex on one of the Polynesian islands. At the time the events in the story occurred, Scott's life was not going well. His marriage of more than twenty years had ended in a bitter divorce, and much too soon he re-married on the rebound to a very pretty, considerably younger woman.

The story is especially remarkable because many Polynesians, particularly in the Hawaiian Islands, have a resentment toward whites that is similar to that of some Native Americans on the mainland. Their grievances are similar. The populations of both groups were decimated by diseases introduced by American and European visitors. Neither the Native Americans nor the Polynesians had strong alcohol, so they had not developed cultural practices to defend against it. It has had a devastating effect on both of those indigenous cultures. Even the mosquito was unknown in Hawaii until the *Wellington* landed on Maui in 1826.

Considering that background, Scott's story is all the more stunning:

The Kahuna

We were going through money faster than we should have. When I asked Bobbie about it, she would say things are just expensive here. Some mornings she would have a hard time waking up, and I started to get suspicious. Then I had to go to a three-day meeting on the mainland for the job. When I got back, Bobbie wasn't there, and everything of value in the house was gone. Both the checking account and the savings account were wiped out.

Two failed marriages and I felt like shit. I started drinking, and that didn't help. About midnight I said, "Fuck it," and decided to kill myself. I figured the easiest way to do it was to swim out from the island until I was exhausted and let the current take me. I went down to the beach, but decided to sit down on the sand for a few minutes before going into the water.

While I was sitting there an old guy came up. He looked native Hawaiian and wore that wrap-around thing. He said, "I know what you're thinking. Can I sit down for a few minutes?" I said, "Sure." He sat next to me, and we talked for about two hours.

While we talked, I changed my mind. I thanked him and went home to get a little sleep before going to work. Two of the guys on my crew were mostly Polynesian, and I called them over. I didn't tell them I had planned to kill myself. I told them I had some problems and I met an old guy on the beach last night who helped me out. They both said, "You met the Kahuna." I told them I'd like to

MYSTICAL EXPERIENCES

thank him and asked them how to find the guy. They said, "You can't find him. He finds you."

I asked Scott what it was like talking to the Kahuna, and he said, "It was like talking to a therapist who has ESP." Scott added that a few years after Bobbie left him, he hired a private detective to find out what had happened to her. He found that she had died of a drug overdose.

In Hawaii I learned that the word "Kahuna" means a person who has achieved mastery in a particular area. A champion surfer or a top-notch boat builder can also be called a Kahuna, but the Kahuna in this story excelled at healing. Scott is the type of man who becomes determined once he makes a decision. I believe that he would have killed himself if the Kahuna had not intervened. I feel sure that the Kahuna saved Scott's life. Whether by cues from Scott's body language or by ESP, but more likely a combination of both, the Kahuna learned of Scott's distress. He must have felt empathy for Scott and was moved to intervene. The racial difference did not stop him. It has been my observation that true healers seem not to even notice racial differences. The enlightened know we are all interconnected.

The Kahuna came from the shamanic tradition, a healing system that goes back to the Stone Age. There are petroglyphs and cave paintings on all the inhabited continents that depict shamans. I have seen many in the U.S. Southwest as well as in both the Sierra de la Giganta and the Sierra de Guadalupe mountain ranges of Mexico. The anthropologist Michael Harner has done remarkable work reviving the healing techniques of shamans. A particularly interesting technique, called Soul Retrieval, was revived by Harner and one of his students, Sandra Ingerman.

In shamanism there is no distinction between physical and emotional illness. The view is that if a person needs healing, he or she needs healing. It is also believed that if a person suffers a trauma, either physical or emotional, he loses a portion of his soul. If a person loses too many portions, he perishes. A task of the shaman is to make a shamanic journey, usually in a trance state achieved through drumming at a particular frequency, and then locate and return the lost portions of the person's soul. On the journey the shaman often calls on helping spirits or power animals for assistance.

This may seem non-credible to the modern reader, but patients have told me remarkable accounts. One patient, Sean, went to one of Dr. Harner's certified shamanic practitioners for a soul retrieval. He had experienced several severe stresses. Two psychiatrists, Thomas Holmes and Richard Rahe, have developed a scale to quantify stress, particularly the stresses that precede a major physical illness. On their scale Sean was off the chart. Within six weeks he had been let go from his job due to a downsizing, his wife had asked for a divorce, he had to find a new residence and move, his closest friend was dying of melanoma, and a family member was found to have a serious illness. This is Sean's account:

A Shamanic Soul Retrieval

When I went for the appointment, the shaman had me lie on the floor on an exercise mat, and he gave me a bandana to put over my eyes. He began drumming with a monotonous beat. After about fifteen minutes he sank down on another exercise pad and laid there for a while. Then he came over to me and sat me up. Next he breathed onto the top of my head at that place where babies have the soft spot.

The shaman said that he had found two pieces of my soul that he returned to me when he breathed onto my head. One piece had been lost when I had gotten a bad burn, and the other was from an emotional thing that happened when I was a kid. What blew my mind, though, was he described the places where both things happened, and he described them exactly.

It is interesting that the shaman did not deal with any of Sean's immediate problems, but helped resolve the effects of earlier traumas. This made Sean stronger in a number of ways, and it gave him greater confidence. The soul retrieval increased his power to deal with the current stresses. The shaman also gave Sean good advice. He told him to hang out with good friends and find an accepting group or community. On his own Sean decided to enter psychotherapy. He did not become physically sick, although the stress research would have predicted a serious illness.

Within a few months Sean found a better job than the one he had lost. He got into shape physically, and within two years he found a beautiful woman who was emotionally healthier than the ex-wife who had dumped him. When Sean finished psychotherapy, his quality of life was far better than before he was hit by the series of disasters.

It is notable that Sean's progress began with soul retrieval, a spiritual experience. Some holy men in India—for example, Sri Siva—believe that psychological growth, and even physical improvement such as weight loss, flow much better when they are preceded by spiritual work. I believe that was the case with Sean. He worked hard in therapy, his progress was rapid, and he also got in shape physically. I believe that the spiritual work facilitated his progress in the other areas.

In addition to shamanism, in recent decades a number of ancient healing techniques have re-appeared to complement standard medical treatment. These include healing touch, which is widely practiced among nurses as well as others; Reiki, a technique from the Buddhist tradition; and bio-energy healing, effected by energy projection. The approach used by this last group is related to the Qi Gong tradition in China. I am particularly impressed by the bio-energy healers, and I have seen remarkable results.

One of the best known healers is a Canadian young man who goes by the pseudonym Adam Dreamhealer. Ronnie Hawkins, the legendary musician who immigrated to Canada from Arkansas in the 1950s, was diagnosed with terminal pancreatic cancer in 2002.

Pancreatic cancer is a deadly one; the prognosis is poor, and depression is often a side effect. Adam began treating Hawkins from a distance on September 21, 2002. On February 27, 2003, there was no evidence of a tumor on a CT scan.

Edgar Mitchell, the scientist and former astronaut, was diagnosed with kidney cancer in 2003. That cancer also has a poor prognosis. Adam worked on Mitchell from Canada while Mitchell lived in the U.S. The treatment lasted from December 2003 until June 2004, when in Mitchell's words, "the irregularity was gone and we haven't seen it since." What form of energy can be transmitted from a healer in Canada, and be effective in healing a patient over 1,000 miles away? That healing energy obviously does not follow the pattern of other forms of energy, where the strength diminishes in proportion to the square of the distance.

This healing energy also appears to be related to the energy that is activated in acupuncture. Several of my psychotherapy patients have also had acupuncture. Ron made a great deal of money and then threw it away when he became addicted to cocaine. He credits both treatments in helping him beat his addiction. He said that acupuncture stopped the craving, but he also needed psychotherapy to learn to deal with his emotions and work through some painful issues.

Ron, as well as others who have had acupuncture, report that they feel energy moving around in their bodies when the needles are inserted. This energy goes by various names: *Prana* in India, *Ki* in Japan, *Chi* or *Qi* in China, depending on the area, and *Mana* in Hawaii and other Pacific islands. Well over a dozen patients have told me they feel this energy move around in their bodies when they have acupuncture. Although scientists have not been able to directly measure the energy, one healer has worked with reputable scientists to demonstrate the effects of bio-energy. Their results have been published in reputable peer-reviewed scientific journals.

MYSTICAL EXPERIENCES

Mietek Wirkus is a healer who immigrated to the U.S. from Poland and now practices in the greater Washington, D.C. area. Mietek does not claim to diagnose or treat diseases. He says that he works on a patient's bio-energy field, balancing it and eliminating blockages. With these corrections, a patient's own healing abilities will often produce recovery, or speed recovery when used in combination with medical treatment. Mietek said that he would become exhausted after working on patients for a short time when he was a young man. Later, a Buddhist monk showed him breathing techniques to use while working. With these techniques Mietek says that he can now work hours at a time without undue fatigue.

Some studies of Mietek's effectiveness have been done on human cells in the test tube, which eliminates the problem of the placebo effects that occur when dealing with people. In a particularly interesting experiment conducted at Walter Reed Army Institute for Research, Mietek projected energy that increased calcium concentration in human cultured Jurkat T cells. This is important because calcium concentration is involved in many cell functions, including metabolism, growth, hormone secretion, gene expression and protein synthesis.

Additional evidence that more than placebo effects are involved in bio-energy healing comes from China, where Chi Gong healers often work on sick or injured farm animals. Owners of farm animals are pragmatic. They would not pay Chi Gong healers to work on their animals if they did not see positive results.

Chapter Eight

The Dark Arts:
Destructive Uses of Psychic Energy

Psychic powers can be developed through concentration and meditation, and control over bodily processes can be acquired through yoga or modern biofeedback. Early in my career I made an assumption that people who achieved these abilities through hard work and discipline had benevolent intentions. That is not always true. Donald Powell Wilson, who spent three years working at Ft. Leavenworth, published in 1951 what has become a classic, *My Six Convicts*. In it he told of Hadad, a man who developed psychic abilities rivaling those in fictional accounts. Yet Hadad was evil and had been involved in multiple murders.

Hadad hypnotized guards without their being aware of it. He caused one guard to give over his belt and made the guard hallucinate that his belt was still on his waist. When the guard later realized what had happened, he was so traumatized he requested a transfer. Hadad used the belt to fake suicide, reducing his metabolism and heartbeat to the point that a medical officer pronounced him dead. He maintained this state for three days. When the physicians were about to make an incision for an autopsy, Hadad sat up and said, "Gentlemen, I would rather not, if you don't mind."

The prison hospital contained men with severe neurological problems that caused frequent convulsions. Medication could not control the convulsions for even a day, but Hadad boasted that he could stop the convulsions on that ward for three days. The convulsions did stop for three days and resumed at the hour Hadad had predicted. During the entire time Hadad was in a solitary confinement cell. Hadad's misuse of his abilities was a tragedy. He could have been a renowned healer, but he wasted his talent.

The things of this world can be used for either positive or negative purposes, and this is also true of energy. Witchcraft and Voodoo are both legitimate religions, but have garnered bad reputations. I am more knowledgeable about witchcraft because I have had several Wiccan patients over the years. Many times Wiccans are treated badly because of their religion. They are accused of worshipping Satan, but they do not even believe in Satan. They actually worship nature, as well as both a god and a goddess who represent the male and female aspects of the universe. I know of no modern Wiccan who would even consider using a spell to harm someone, but there do exist ancient *grimoires*, or books of spells that contain instructions for harming people.

As the anthropologist and ethnobotanist Wade Davis has shown, Voodoo is a religion as sophisticated as most other religions. Unfortunately *The Serpent and the Rainbow*, a Hollywood movie made about his work in Haiti, distorted his findings. The Voodoo religion derives from the West African religions of slaves brought to Haiti and also incorporates some elements of Catholicism. Because slaves could not have their own police force to punish those who did evil in their community, the harmful effects of Voodoo were developed as a form of social control to keep order in their society.

Davis proved that zombies are real. They are not the "walking dead" of horror movies; they are people who were punished for serious destructive behavior which the community found intolerable. People who are zombies have been poisoned by the clandestine administration of two toxins; the first derived from a poisonous fish, and the second from a plant in the datura family. The first poison puts the person in an extremely low metabolic state where-

MYSTICAL EXPERIENCES

by no breath is detected. The townspeople assume that the person has died, and the person is buried. After three days those who administered the poison dig the zombie up. Then the second toxin is administered.

As a result of three days with insufficient oxygen, plus the toxins, the zombie is brain damaged. Afterwards the zombie is compliant, rather fearful, and unable to do complex tasks. They are used only for unskilled labor such as cane cutting. It is easy to see why people believe that zombies are the walking dead. Fear of being made into a zombie is a powerful incentive to behave in a just manner.

Although there is nothing occult or paranormal about zombies, there are powerful occult spells within Voodoo. These spells can do harm through the negative use of energy. Tyrone, an African-American young man from inner-city Baltimore, told me the following story:

The Haitian Book

I was hungry so I went to this 7-11 store for some food. This homeless guy was sitting on the sidewalk out front and he looked like he was in bad shape, starving and maybe ready to die. When I got my stuff, I figured I'd get something for him too. I gave him a box of cookies and a Coke. He acted real happy and got all excited. I couldn't understand what he was saying. It sounded French, and he didn't speak English. He took a little book out of his bag and gave it to me. He showed me this design in the book; he pointed to it and made noises. I couldn't understand him, but I didn't have to. Somehow I just knew what it was and what to do with it.

After my mother died, my aunt, her sister, took me and my little sister in. She was nice, but her boyfriend who lived with her wasn't. When she wasn't around he'd beat us. One day he beat me real bad, so I got the book out. I don't know how, but I knew which design to use. I stared at the design for a long time, more than a couple of hours, while I thought about him getting hurt. The next day he fell down the stairs and broke his leg.

There was a teacher at school who was fucking with me. He'd ask me to read in front of the class a lot, and I hated that. I couldn't read good and I didn't want the class to see it. He'd make fun of me when I made mistakes, too. I used the book on him. He got hurt in a car accident and had to be out for a couple of months.

When I heard about his accident, I started getting real antsy and scared of the book. I wrapped it up in plastic and buried it. A few weeks later I got locked up on this armed robbery charge.

Tyrone told me where he had buried the book and asked me to get it for him. I declined. I tried to teach Tyrone about negative energy. It boomerangs back on people when they use magic to harm others. I cautioned him to only use magic for positive purposes, and I hope that I got through to him.

In earlier times almost every culture had similar procedures for killing an enemy by magical means. An interesting one from the Inuit culture involves an evil charm called a *tupilait* or *tupilaq*. This has been documented by several Arctic explorers, and more recently by scholars at Nunavit Arctic College in Canada. The college has a fascinating program of interviewing tribal elders in the Arctic to record knowledge of earlier beliefs and practices.

A *tupilaq* is a small sculpture of an evil spirit, usually carved in bone or walrus ivory and about two inches high. The person using the charm, usually an *angakoq* or shaman, performed rituals to give it power, and sent it to kill an adversary. On those occasions when one was sent against a person of great spiritual power, that person could turn it around. Then the *tupilaq* would return and kill the maker. Greenland was a Danish colony for many years. By chance I noticed a *tupilaq* in the window of a Copenhagen pawnshop. I bought it at a reasonable price, but I am not about to use it to harm anyone.

MYSTICAL EXPERIENCES

The most common way to kill an enemy by magic across cultures has involved death poems. Most often the procedure used a rhyming chant or poem accompanied by a ritual. The rituals differ depending on the culture, but the specifics of the ritual are not important. The purpose of ritual and the chanted verse is to focus the mind without distraction. This concentrates the energy coming from the person doing the spell, and the contents of the chant direct the energy to the victim.

These deadly chants or poems are usually known by the familiar term "satires" when translated, but most ancient cultures had two kinds of satire, one intended to embarrass, and one intended to kill. In ancient Greece, even Plato was convinced deadly satire worked. He thought it was even more effective if the verse was in iambic form. In his work *The Laws*, in which he tried to develop an ideal legal framework for a utopian state, he prohibited the use of deadly satire. If a person used deadly satire in iambic form, Plato prescribed immediate banishment without benefit of trial. The deadly satire of ancient Greece contained mockery and ridicule like conventional satire, but it also contained a self-confident tone, a will that the enemy die, a sense of outraged justice, and strong hatred.

There are many examples of deadly satire in the old literature of the Celtic peoples, especially that of Ireland and Wales. A story from pre-Christian Ireland tells of Caier, king of Connacht, in the western part of the country. Caier had a much younger and dissatisfied wife who had her eye on Nede, a poet. Nede began reciting deadly verse to kill Caier. It was effective. Caier woke one morning with large blisters on his face, and he died soon afterward.

Nede paid a heavy price for his success. The old manuscript says that when Caier died, a rock exploded and a piece of the stone hit Nede under the eye and "pierced into his head," killing him. The exploding rock is an important detail, because heating a river stone in a fire was part of the required ritual. As those who do much camping know, this is dangerous. Experienced campers use dry stones around a fire because river stones have often absorbed water. When heated, high pressure steam can build up in the stone and cause it to explode.

There are many examples of deadly verse from around the world, but I find the following Cherokee spell particularly chilling:

A Spell to Destroy a Life

> Listen!
> I know your name.
> I know your clan.
> I have stolen your spirit and buried it under earth.
> I cover your soul under earth.
> I cover you over with black rock.
> I cover you over with black cloth.
> I cover you over with black slabs.
> You disappear forever.
> Your path leads to the black coffin in the hills of the Darkening Land.
> So let it be for you.
> The black clay of the Darkening Land.
> Your soul fades away.
> It becomes blue.
> When darkness comes your spirit shrivels and dwindles to disappear forever.
> Listen!
>
> Translated by James Mooney

Destructive spells and sorcery continue to be used within aboriginal communities in Australia. Occasionally the victims are rescued by white Australians and brought to a hospital for treatment. Donald Eastlake, one of Australia's "flying doctors," or physicians who pilot small aircraft to provide medical services to remote areas, has said that the victims of sorcery usually have a profound hopelessness. They have given up to the extent that they do not even

MYSTICAL EXPERIENCES

bother to consume food or water. Eastlake said the victims suffer from severe dehydration, and large amounts of fluid are needed to restore normal body processes and kidney function. Eastlake does not consider whether or not the concentrated thoughts of the person casting the spell have power to harm. The studies of Qi Gong healers indicate that thoughts have the power to heal, so it is not a leap to say that they also have the power to harm.

About a decade ago I considered writing a book on those destructive verses and spells meant to harm others. In my draft I emphasized a cross-cultural approach, and in no part did I include both the complete verse and the required ritual; it was always one or the other. I sent inquiries to a few agents. One responded, a woman with a solid track record of placing books with good publishing houses. Rather than her office, she set up our meeting at a nearby restaurant. It was a beautiful late-spring day, so tables were set in the adjacent garden for *al fresco* dining. The smell of spring was in the air, the food and the setting were delightful, and the woman was pretty, charming, quite intelligent. I had an enjoyable lunch.

After the meal she dropped the bomb. She told me she would represent the book on the condition that I teach her one of the spells, including both the verse and the ritual that went with it. The agent told me the name of the intended victim, a writer who had burned her in some kind of scam. While I did not know the writer personally, I knew of her reputation for deceit. I believe the agent had a genuine grievance, but I did not want to pay the price for using psychic power to harm others. Not only did I decline the agent's offer, I decided not to write the proposed book.

It is not worth the price of using the power of the mind to harm others. Michael Harner, the previously mentioned anthropologist who studied shamans in many cultures, has said that shamans who work only to help others tend to have long, healthy and fulfilled lives. Those shamans who use their power to harm others tend to die young and have rather unpleasant deaths.

David St. Clair, who studied psychic powers and healers in Brazil, relates a chilling story. A Brazilian woman had a lucrative business as a psychic "killer for hire." When she was paid to harm someone, she never failed, and the victim died within days. Of course, she could not be prosecuted because police had no way to link her to the death. One time she began the ritual to kill a client's enemy. As she was directing the negative energy, the mental image of her only son sprang into her mind. Within a couple of days her son was run over by a truck.

I wonder if Tyrone, the young man who used the Haitian book to harm both his aunt's boyfriend and his teacher, would have committed the crime that sent him to prison if he had not been sending negative energy. The energy sent out to harm others reverts to the sender.

Part Four

Welcome to the Mystery

Chapter Nine

Our World Is Far More Mysterious Than We Realize

David Lewis, Jr., a Muskogee-Creek medicine man, has said, "What the modern educated man fails to recognize is that there are a great many things that he does not know that are in the unseen worlds of creation."

His point is correct. We fail to see some of the marvels of our world, and much of what we take for granted is untrue. We assume that we are stationary, yet we are on a planet zooming through space at 66,000 miles per hour. We assume that thoughts are insubstantial and regard matter as the basic stuff of the world. Like Helmholtz and other nineteenth-century scientists, we believe that matter is permanent and can only be changed in form. We also believe that when energy is transmitted, the power decreases in proportion to the square of the distance. Yet many of these commonly held assumptions are false.

Many modern Americans who cite nineteenth-century science in their objections to parapsychology also use digital cameras. They are unaware their cameras are based on quantum mechanics and utilize work that led to two Nobel prizes. The purpose of the chapters in this section is to explore the assumptions and also the mysteries of our world. Our world is larger, more mysterious and more fun than we realize.

Human thoughts have power. Dr. Masaru Emoto has shown that human vibrational energy, thoughts, words, ideas and music affect the molecular structure of water. In his experiments he freezes drops of water and then examines them using dark-field photography. In one experiment words were written on pieces of paper which were then taped to jars of water. Words like "You make me sick. I will kill you," produced non-symmetrical, disturbed crystals, but words such as "Thank you" or an expression of love, gratitude or appreciation produced beautiful, symmetrical crystals. Water blessed by a Buddhist monk also produced beautiful crystals. This work is important because our bodies are more than 80 percent water. It is likely that symmetrical molecules can pass through the cell membranes of our bodies more easily than jagged asymmetrical ones and thus replenish us more effectively.

It turns out that many of our assumptions about the world are simply not true. We assume that matter is basic stuff, and the form of matter can be changed, but it cannot be created or destroyed. This assumption does not stand up to the discoveries of modern physics. Atoms are the building blocks of matter, but atoms are mostly space. The particles of the atom are only a tiny proportion of the total.

To make circumstance even more strange, the electrons of atoms pop in and out of existence. Even the nucleus can disappear and later reappear. Where do they go when they disappear? Some have proposed a parallel universe. Werner Heisenberg, who posited the uncertainty principle, has said, "Atoms are not things, they are only possibilities."

Modern physics became quite different from classical physics when the principle of non-locality was developed. Non-locality states that if two elementary particles such as electrons or photons come from a common source, they are entangled even though they travel away from each other at the speed of light. In the words of Russell Targ, "If you grab one, the other shows the effect of that."

MYSTICAL EXPERIENCES

This effect occurs with no exchange of force or energy. This means that the physical world is a complex web of interdependent relationships. This may also apply to humans. The principle of non-locality with particles parallels a belief within Hinduism about people. If a couple with strong mutual affection makes love, there is a connection between them for the rest of their lives, even if they go separate ways.

Another principle of modern physics is that observing events affects the outcome. In other words, particles are only possibilities until they are observed. Things can get weird with this principle. Erwin Schrodinger proposed a thought experiment whereby a cat is put in a box with a Geiger counter, a radioactive atom that may or may not decay, and a fatal dose of poison that will be released if the atom indeed decays. He asks the question, "Is the cat alive or dead?" The cat is both alive and dead until the box is opened. The act of observing will render the cat either alive or dead.

While I do not claim to understand much of quantum physics, it is interesting to note that experts in the field, such as Fred Alan Wolf, Russell Targ and Hal Putoff, see no contradiction between science and many paranormal phenomena including ESP, remote viewing, telepathy, precognitive dreams, and spiritual healing either locally or from a distance.

Psychic energy is independent of distance. As noted in the earlier chapter on healing, the healing energy projected to Edgar Mitchell by a Canadian healer from more than 1,000 miles away was effective. People have had ESP experiences in which they knew of something happening to someone they love thousands of miles away. Dr. Masaru Emoto has also noted that distance does not seem to matter in his experiments with water.

Chapter Ten

ESP and Paranormal Phenomena

When a soldier in World War I, Hans Berger, was injured, his family sent a telegram to learn if he was badly hurt. Berger saw the time the telegram was sent and found it was almost immediately after the injury. After inquiring, he found that his family knew of the injury through ESP. Berger assumed that electromagnetic energy went from his brain to a family member, probably his sister. After the war he began research on the electromagnetic energy emitted by the brain. He failed to find the energy involved in ESP, but his work led to the development of the electroencephalogram, or EEG, which became an important diagnostic tool in medicine.

There are a vast number of examples of ESP, but the topic still does not have scientific respectability. Over lunch I asked a psychologist colleague whether he believed in ESP. He said, "I'm agnostic about it." After we talked for about an hour, he told me of two dramatic examples of ESP in his personal life. He is a bright, insightful guy, yet he did not see the inconsistency in his comments.

Jacob Cohen (1923-1998) was a psychologist at New York University for many years and author of a textbook on statistical analysis in the behavioral sciences. He said that there is more experimental evidence supporting ESP than there is for many of the principles presented as fact in standard psychology textbooks.

In light of Cohen's assertion, why isn't ESP more widely accepted? There are two reasons. The first is that ESP violates many people's idea about how the universe works. Most people assume that time is linear, like traveling down a one-way street. The past is gone, the present is now, and we can only make probability judgments about the future. We cannot view the future. I do not claim to understand time, but when Blanche saw an event two years in my future, I knew the linear model had to be wrong. Another problem involves energy transfer. In the sending of all known forms of energy, the energy degrades over distance. Yet distance does not seem to make a difference in ESP or in the transmission of healing energy.

The second major reason most people do not accept ESP or other paranormal phenomena is that the events often cannot be repeated on demand. Most people with some knowledge of science expect to replicate findings if the same procedures are used, but this is not the case with ESP. The purpose of this chapter is to explore the objections to ESP and show that ESP is fully compatible with modern science.

Consider the following example of ESP, one which violates our assumptions regarding time. The story comes from Ramon, a pharmacologist now seventy years of age. He grew up in the U.S. in a bilingual home and is fluent in Spanish and English. Ramon obtained his B.A. from a U.S. university, but he decided to study in Spain for his advanced degrees.

The Spanish Fortune Teller

At the university I met Pilar. We started going out and she became my girlfriend. We were walking through the city one day and passed the booth of a *bruja*, a fortune teller. I didn't even pay her a fee, she just started talking to us. She said, "You two will get married and you will have one child, a son." Then she turned to me and said, "You will enjoy good health for most of your life, but when you get old, you will have pain in your legs and feet."

Now seventy years of age, Ramon says that the fortune teller's predictions came true. He married Pilar and they have a son. He also has a painful case of arthritis in his legs and feet which acts up in rainy weather. Ramon says he can predict coming rain better than the Weather Bureau.

Like Blanche seeing me working for the state two years before it happened, this is an example of ESP occurring in non-linear time. The fortune teller's prediction was almost forty years before Ramon developed arthritis. It is unlikely that the fortune teller could see signs of arthritis in Ramon's gait that early, so he is convinced she had a gift.

Both anecdotal and experimental evidence for ESP is so abundant that additional examples are unnecessary. The important question is, under what conditions does it occur? There is evidence for two factors. The Canadian neuroscientist Michael Persinger and the American psychologist Stanley Krippner have found that ESP is more likely to occur when the earth's geo-magnetic field is calm, and when there are few electric storms or sun spots. A calm mind is the second factor, and particularly important because it is key in replicating ESP and other paranormal events.

When measured on the electroencephalogram, or EEG, waking brain activity falls under two categories, Beta and Alpha. The faster wave is Beta, about 13 to 30 Hz or cycles per second. These waves are low in amplitude and irregular in shape when plotted on a chart or oscilloscope. Beta occurs when we are alert, activated, excited, attentive or working on a problem. Alpha waves are slower, about 8 to 12 Hz, but higher in amplitude. Alpha occurs when we are calm and quiet, or relaxing. It can be enhanced by closing the eyes.

In my first encounter with a psychic, Blanche, she spent about fifteen minutes prior to the session chatting and telling me about her children. She did more of the talking, and I was careful not to divulge personal details of my life. We both relaxed, and it seemed that we both entered an Alpha state. I believe this facilitated her abilities during the session. Inmates who have disclosed ESP experiences to me have used various expressions to describe the same thing, such as the inmate who stared at his cigarette lighter to "go into a zone."

The psychologist Charles Tart has noted the importance of Alpha for ESP. Tart has advocated that psychological research become "state specific." In other words, experiments should include a procedure to ensure that research volunteers are in the state most appropriate for the topic under investigation. Although Tart's suggestion has not caught on, an interesting incident supports his case. For many years Professor J.B. Rhine conducted research on ESP at Duke University. He had student volunteers guess which of five designs, each one printed on a card, was the design that either Rhine or his assistant was trying to mentally project. His results tended to have statistical significance, but the size of the effect was relatively small.

José Silva said that he contacted Rhine and suggested the use of relaxation exercises prior to experiments to put the volunteers in an Alpha state. A stuffy academic, Rhine did not take Silva seriously because Silva lacked a Ph.D. That was a mistake. Despite the lack of university degrees, Silva had a genius-level intellect, and his suggestion would have made Rhine's work far more impressive. It is possible to get statistical significance with a small effect when there is a large sample of people in experiments. Silva's suggestion would have added an impressive larger effect, making Rhine's work more noteworthy.

Silva had no academic degrees because he was born into poverty in Laredo, on the Texas-Mexico border. Since he had to work as a child to help support his family, he had no formal schooling until he went into the U. S. Army during World War II. The Army trained him as a radio repairman, and that was the extent of his formal education. Despite that beginning, Silva wrote two books and earned two patents for electrical devices. Silva also founded Silva Mind Control, and although the name sounds strange, it was the most successful of the modern self-help movements.

MYSTICAL EXPERIENCES

Silva believed that in addition to ESP, an Alpha state facilitates many types of learning. This is especially true in learning foreign languages. During a one-week course in Spanish using an Alpha state taught by Judith Serrano, I learned far more than I would have in a traditional classroom. She played Baroque music in the background during the classes, particularly Vivaldi's *Four Seasons* and Pacabel's *Canon*. While I could not expect to become fluent in a week, I learned enough Spanish to get by during trips to Latin America.

Since Rhine's death, other researchers, including Charles Honorton and Richard Broughton, have shown that larger effects could be produced by reducing the amount of sensory stimuli reaching the research volunteers in ESP experiments. In their experiments both Honorton and Broughton used a technique called "*ganzfeld*," which means "entire field" in German. In this technique half of a ping pong ball is taped over each eye to reduce visual stimulation to a diffuse, soft light. A white noise generator produces a soft hissing sound to mask auditory noise, and the volunteer sits in a plush reclining chair to reduce touch sensation. In those experiments correct guess produced hit rates of 34 percent, when chance would have predicted a hit rate of 25 percent.

All the great religions have emphasized quieting the mind through meditation, contemplation, and mantra-like prayer. The Buddha made meditation one of the steps in his eight-fold path. Approximately 2,200 years ago the Hindu sage and physician Patanjali emphasized quieting the mind by concentrating on a candle flame, a flower or a mantra to reach a higher state of awareness. There are also many examples in Islam and in the Judeo-Christian traditions. The early Christian fathers went out into the desert to meditate and pray free of distraction. The Catholic saint Juan de la Cruz urged people to still the surface mind to reach a deeper level of wisdom.

When we quiet the mind, amazing things happen. Jason told me the following story:

The Lottery

I got up at six to mediate for twenty minutes before getting ready for work. I did everything as usual and repeated my mantra, but the thought of the number 4-4-4 kept coming to mind for the whole twenty minutes. When the timer dinged, I figured I just didn't have a good meditation that day.

Later in the evening when we finished supper, my son John asked if he could be excused and left the room to watch TV. My wife and I stayed at the table talking. A few minutes later John came back and said, "Hey, Dad. A funny number just won the lottery. It was 4-4-4." I had not told John about my meditation, and of course I hadn't thought of buying a lottery ticket.

Meditation teachers warn against trying to have an experience like Jason's, which they call *siddhis*. They say to accept if it happens, but do not look for it. That makes sense. Trying to do something will put you in a Beta rather than Alpha state.

Another fascinating tale of ESP was revealed by Jimmy Carter in 1995. Decades earlier a plane of military significance went down in the jungles of Zaire, now called Congo, and both American and Russian groups were searching for it. The Americans found it first through a technique known as "remote viewing." In that technique a person goes into a deeply relaxed state and tries to visualize the particular location. An American visualized and described the location so well the CIA was able to determine the site and sent their team in. They got there before the Russians.

It is interesting that in European folktales magical things, like visits from fairies, happen to women when they are at their spinning wheel. For centuries spinning flax or wool into yarn to make clothing was an evening chore for European women. Before the twentieth century, when electric lighting became available, candles were expensive and most people used them only for special occasions. Rooms were dark in the evening, especially during the long winters in northern Europe. The living room or kitchen was illuminated only by the glow from the hearth. The monotonous spin of the wheel must have been relaxing in the semi-darkness, but the woman had to constantly feed wool into the wheel and keep the wheel spinning. This would keep her from dozing off into a sleep state, and the result was that they spent long periods in Alpha, which is conducive for paranormal experiences.

An Air Force officer friend told me of an interesting experience when he was in a deeply relaxed state, but awake rather than asleep. He had been on a flight above cloud cover for hours when he saw a scantily clad girl walk across his radar screen. Similarly, Charles Lindberg saw spirits in the cockpit on his lonely flight across the Atlantic.

It is difficult to repeat ESP on demand, but it would happen more often if experimenters put their volunteers into Alpha. The core problem in replicating ESP is that it is a weak signal. Those of us who grew up in the era of AM radio know about weak signals getting through competing noise. We could hear only local stations during daylight hours because there was too much electronic noise and too many other stations broadcasting, and atmospheric conditions were also better after sundown. Late at night we could hear stations from far away locations. In New England where I grew up, we could hear country music from stations in Tennessee and other distant states.

A colleague told me of an experience illustrating that fewer competing stimuli or less "noise" facilitates ESP. Early in his career as a psychologist, Paul went through psychotherapy himself. Much of it was in the classic Freudian style, lying on a couch with closed eyes while free associating, although this technique is uncommon these days. As one session began Paul was reminded to free associate and tell the first thought that came into his mind.

Paul did so, and his first thought was "apricots." His analyst was startled. That morning she and her husband had talked at great length about apricots. They were growing fruit trees on their small farm, but were having difficulty. Apricots can take extremes of temperature, but not fluctuations. As a result, they are hard to grow in Maryland. The analyst and her husband had thought they were finally going to get a good crop, but had lost all their fruit the night before. When trees carry fruit they cannot support, "June drop" occurs and immature fruit falls to the ground. Lying on the couch with closed eyes, Paul picked up on the thoughts of his therapist and her husband.

Another argument against ESP is that no one has gotten James Randi's money. A one million dollar prize has been offered by James Randi to anyone who demonstrates ESP or other paranormal ability at his laboratory. Randi put up $10,000, and a foundation added $990,000.

Some background on Randi is important to understand why no one has won the prize. Born Randall James Hamilton Zwinge in Ontario, he adopted the stage name James "The Amazing" Randi for his career as stage magician. He retired at age sixty, thereafter becoming a professional debunker of claims of paranormal ability, although Randi prefers to call himself an investigator. To cite an example, Randi seems to have a particular gripe about homeopathic medicine. The Internet carries a video of Randi ridiculing the assumptions of homeopathic practitioners in front of an audience, evoking much laughter. He fails to address the only important questions: do homeopathic remedies work, and are there serious side effects?

I do not necessarily advocate the homeopathic approach; I have tried only one such product. My wife and I live in the Appalachian Mountains of western Maryland, only minutes from the Appalachian Trail. We do a lot of hiking, trail running and some nontechnical climbing. Of course, this results in occasional falls and bruises. I have used the homeopathic remedy for bruises, and it seems to work. There is less bruising and the marks do not last as long. I fully realize that this does not approach the requirements of a controlled clinical trial, but it seems that additional well-controlled tests of the homeopathic approach are necessary. Randi's sarcasm about homeopathic remedies is not relevant to the central question of whether or not they work.

Jacques Benveniste (1935-2004), a respected French immunologist, conducted a series of experiments on the effects of a homeopathic substance on basophils. Basophils are granular leukocytes, one of the cell types involved in the immune response. He submitted a paper with the results of his experiments to the scientific journal *Nature* in 1988. The editors at *Nature* were puzzled by his results, because they thought the homeopathic agent was too dilute to account for the biological effects. They agreed to publish the paper only if the experiments were repeated at an independent laboratory with observers. The observers included the editor of *Nature*, Sir John Maddox, and the ex-stage magician James Randi.

Benveniste said the atmosphere at the independent laboratory was "circus like," with Randi taping papers to the ceiling and doing card tricks during the experiments. Most of the results did not support Benveniste, but two experiments were positive and did support him. Somehow the positive results were ignored, and there were claims that his earlier experiments were "synthetic."

There have been subsequent experiments to test Benveniste's work. Some of the studies with negative results were poorly designed. One study, sponsored by the BBC, actually included a chemical poisonous to basophils. How could they expect to get a favorable response from a homeopathic remedy on cells that were being poisoned? There have been some positive studies. Madeline Ennis, a British research biochemist, said that she began as a skeptic, but the results compelled her to suspend her disbelief. The unfortunate result of the whole affair was that the unfounded suggestion of fraud tarnished the reputation of a good scientist. Afterwards Benveniste had trouble getting funding and had to self-finance some of his research.

More recently George Vithoulkas, a Greek homeopathic practitioner, negotiated for more than two years with Randi's team to set up a study of homeopathy. Vithoulkas lined up a hospital, physicians and a group of patients to participate in the study. The proposed research design was rigorous and double-blind. Half the patients were to get placebos, and the other half homeopathic medicines. This was to be a well-controlled experiment on the effectiveness of homeopathy.

Randi says that Vithoulkas backed out, but Vithoulkas insists it was Randi who did so. Vithoulkas believes that Randi has no intention of participating in a solidly designed experiment where he may have to part with the money. The experiences of Benveniste and Vithoulkas show that it is unlikely any scientist will get the one million dollars and that participating in an attempt will only damage their careers.

There is another group who do not deny that ESP exists, but claim it is unimportant, even trivial compared to other human behaviors and abilities. This view neglects the fact that ESP has survival value. It helps save lives. This is illustrated in the following story told by Jared:

Wiring

I saw a psychic that a friend recommended, and he told me, "You have a problem with your wiring. You better do something about it without wasting any time." I didn't know of any good electricians, so I went over to my friend, Carl. A few months earlier Carl had added an extra room on his house. He had done most of the work himself, but he hired a licensed electrician for the wiring. Carl had told me that the electrician did a good job and his price was reasonable. When I told him about the psychic, Carl laughed and said, "No, Jared, the guy meant this wiring." Carl pointed to his head. He did give me the electrician's phone number, and I made an appointment.

The electrician came to my place and checked everything out. My house was wired for 220 volts, but the electric company only supplied 110. They had spliced two 110 lines together to give me 220, but the splice had loosened. On the back of the plywood panel where the junction box was located, electricity was arcing between the two 110 lines. The back of that plywood panel was badly scorched. If I hadn't gotten it fixed, it was only a matter of time before I would have had a fire.

Jared was right. Without the psychic's warning he quite possibly could have had a fire, and if it had happened at night, the whole family could have been killed. Psychic abilities are not trivial. They have great survival value.

Jaded told an interesting aside about the psychic. He said that the psychic told him that he had a desk job and did not do manual labor. The psychic asked Jared his birth date and said Jared had to be careful of sore throats and take care of them before they led to bronchitis. He also advised Jared to make time in his life for contact with nature.

Jared felt the psychic had a gift, but the gift was not used for all the observations. Jared is a bit overweight and his hands are free of calluses. Any observant person could tell he did not do manual labor. The other two comments are based on popular astrology. Jared's birth date is at the end of April, making him a Taurus. Astrologists believe Taurus people have a weakness for lower respiratory diseases and they have a need to spend time with nature. Some astrologists say Taurus people will die without some exposure to nature, even if it is only taking care of houseplants in an urban environment. Obviously the psychic used a mix of real ability and other sources of information. Some people jump to the conclusion that a psychic is a fraud when they see a mundane source was used for some of the observations. Jared's experience shows that a psychic might have a genuine ability, but also use information from other sources.

Chapter Eleven

The Relationship Between People and Animals

I was invited to participate in a Native American ritual. It began with prayers, and the pipe was passed. When the pipe reached each of us, we took a puff, and then we offered the prayer: "To all my relations." "All my relations" means all our fellow creatures; not just people, but also the animals, plants, rocks, streams, mountains and the earth itself. To the traditional Native American, we are all interrelated. This prayer, accompanied by the use of the pipe, is sacred to traditional Native Americans, as sacred as the sacraments are to Christians.

Most indigenous cultures—for example, traditional Australian aborigines—also believe that all creation is interrelated. A central tenet of shamanism, the first religion of most ethnic groups, is that *everything that is, is alive.* Now only a minority of Japanese formally practice the ancient Shinto religion, where aspects of nature, such as streams, mountains, springs and caves, are considered alive and revered. Yet remnants of Shinto survive in the daily activities of many modern Japanese, and it is not unusual for a man leaving his office for the day to thank his computer, as well as his office furniture, for supporting him in his work.

In August 2009, Y.E. Yang, a golfer from South Korea, scored an upset when he beat Tiger Woods for the PGA championship. After winning the match, Yang first shook hands with his opponent. Next, he saluted his clubs by raising his golf bag over his head. In contrast, U.S. golfers may curse their clubs or even throw a club after a bad shot or a loss. They never salute the clubs when they do well. Many mental health professionals feel that the Asian practice has a positive side effect by making people feel more connected to their environment and less isolated. Some American writers have a variant on the Asian belief; they believe their manuscripts are alive.

The topic of Section Three of this book is the interconnectedness of people. A case can be made for the interconnectedness of all creation, but that is beyond the scope of this book. The focus of this chapter is the connection between people and animals. Animals are both more aware and more complex than many of us realize. J. Allen Boone, who worked for many years in the Hollywood movie industry, has told fascinating stories of interactions between animals and humans on movie sets.

In the late 1940s and into the '50s, when large-budget Westerns were popular, rattlesnake bites were a problem when filming in desert locations. The numerous Native American extras were almost never bitten, but snake bites were a serious problem for white staff. Boone believes that the snakes picked up the fear and hatred of the whites toward snakes. The snakes did not have a problem with the Native Americans and their "live and let live" attitude toward the serpents.

Len, a patient, was phobic about snakes. After we worked on a systematic desensitization, one of the standard treatments for phobias, he reported a dream:

Snake

I was hiking along a path through jungle in the rain. At the far side of a clearing there was a huge snake, either a python or boa constrictor, coiled around a large branch in a tree. I was afraid to go closer. I just stopped and stared at the snake. The snake looked edgy, like he was afraid of me, too. Then the snake said, "You're afraid of me, and I'm afraid of you. Let's respect each other, give each other space."

That was the end of the dream for Len. After that he was no longer phobic of snakes, but he had a healthy respect and did not take chances.

The next group of stories is about dogs, and I do not claim to understand all the implications of this story told to me by an inmate:

Mother's Dog

My mother had problems after my father left. She worked a lot, she drank too much, and she dated, bringing guys home. I guess she was tryin' to find a new husband. She didn't pay much attention to us kids, but she had this little dog she loved. I loved the dog, but I hated it too because it got the attention I wanted. Sometimes when she wasn't there I gave that dog the blues. Once I beat it real bad.

After I got locked up I had this dream on a Thursday night that I was fallin'. While I was fallin' I passed her dog. It was fallin' too, and it barked at me. I had a funny feeling about that after I woke up. The next Sunday my mother visited me, and her eyes looked like she'd been crying. Her dog died that Thursday night.

Many traditional Native Americans believe that, in addition to their ecological niche, each species of animal also carries a spiritual message for mankind. In their view the role of the dog is to teach us about love. Could the dog have been trying to teach the inmate something about love and forgiveness? The psychologist Jean Houston has told touching stories about dogs aiding her in developing her intuition and spiritual growth.

The next story is not so complex, but it does attest to the awareness of dogs. The story comes from Bernie, a computer programmer. Bernie believes in healing touch, which he learned from his girlfriend, a nurse.

Pinto, the Mexican Dog

I decided to go on a five-day camping trip into the Sierras in Mexico with three buddies. We arranged for a guide who had pack animals, so we only had to carry our daypacks. Juan, the guide, had a small rancho, and we brought our camping gear to his place to get started. That first day it took him about an hour and a half to load the burros. He was careful, making sure the loads were balanced and none of the stuff poked them.

We just hung out in the farmyard while he did that, and I talked with his son, who was about eight. It's fun to practice Spanish with kids; they talk slower and don't use big words. He had this spotted dog named Pinto. All four of us took turns patting him and playing with him. I wasn't sure, but I thought I noticed a slight limp on the dog, so when I patted him, I tried to give him healing energy.

It was one of the best camping trips of my life. We saw fantastic rock formations, wild mountains with tiny settlements in the valleys, and we had cooling dips in watering holes they call *posas*. When we got back to the rancho, Pinto ran up to me, stood on his hind legs, and wrapped his front legs around mine. He wasn't humping my leg the way some dogs do; he just held on for about ten minutes. The other guys had played with him and patted him too, maybe longer than I did, but he ran up to me, clung to my leg, and didn't want to let me go.

It is not clear whether the dog actually felt healing energy from Bernie. He may have picked up on Bernie's kind intention, but either way, the story shows that dogs have more awareness than we recognize.

The meaning of the next story is not so clear. It was told by an inmate.

Road Trip

When I was a kid I went on this road trip to Pennsylvania with my grandfather. We drove through a town, and a big white dog with black and brown spots stood on a corner. About an hour later we went through another town about fifty miles away, and that same dog was on a corner. No way that dog could get there before us, an' no way that dog could have an exact look-alike twin. That's not possible. I thought it was weird, but I didn't say anything. Then my grandfather shook his head and said, "Man, that's some strange shit."

The next story is similar, but more ominous. The man is a professional photographer, not an inmate.

Crater Lake

I had wanted to go to Crater Lake for years, so I packed my cameras and camping gear and drove to Oregon. I got to the park headquarters late in the afternoon and went in to get a back country camping permit. The office was open, the lights were on, but no one was around. I yelled and tried to find someone, but even though the place was open, it was deserted.

When I went back to my car, I had a hard time starting it. That was funny, because I had had a tune-up a few days before, and it had made the trip to Oregon with no problems. I finally got it started but it coughed, sputtered, and ran rough. I got out and opened the hood to see if I could spot anything wrong.

Then I noticed this strange-looking guy right behind me. I hadn't seen or heard him come up. He said, "It wouldn't be a good idea to try to drive that car anywhere today." I looked around and saw this white cocker spaniel sitting on the porch, and I looked at the guy more closely. He looked gaunt as hell, and I wondered if he could be a ghost.

I got in the car, and it was still running rough, but I drove out of there. About twenty-five minutes later I saw a little store and I thought about stopping for a juice or a soda, but the same damn white cocker spaniel was on the porch. I hauled ass out of there and didn't stop until I reached Route 97. Funny thing, as soon as I reached 97, the car ran fine.

I do not claim to understand the meaning of the dogs in the two stories having doubles. Both the inmate and the photographer felt they meant something important. The photographer visiting Oregon wondered if the dog at the store was a message about danger, telling him not to stop, just get the hell out of there.

Rupert Sheldrake, the British scientist, has conducted research on communication between humans and animals. He has written about a soldier who came home to visit his parents on leave for a few days and then headed back to the base. After the soldier left, later that evening the family dog began shivering and whining. The parents wondered if the dog was sick, but they could not quiet the animal.

Then they got a phone call from their son. He had had an accident about eighty miles from home, and his injuries were severe but not life threatening. The parents deduced that the dog had gotten upset at the time of the accident. After the parents spoke to their son on the phone, the dog relaxed and went to sleep. In Sheldrake's database he has more than 100 accounts of dogs responding to a distant accident or death of a human companion, and 51 accounts of similar responses in cats.

There are several published stories about pets finding their owners over long distances. This story is from a personal acquaintance. Elizabeth lived with her beloved dog, Maggie, in Santa Barbara for several years. One summer she decided to take a two-week vacation. She planned to spend the first week in Los Angeles, about 90 miles to the south, and the second week in San Francisco, more than 200 miles to the north. She boarded her dog about 15 miles away, on the other side of the Santa Inez Mountains.

Elizabeth had an enjoyable first week visiting old friends in Los Angeles. She had planned to drive straight through to San Francisco, but as she neared Santa Barbara on the way north, she decided to stop at her home and check on things. Because she was tired, she spent the night at home. Late at night she heard scratching at her door. Maggie was there, covered with dirt and mud. She had escaped from the boarder and crossed the mountains to see Elizabeth.

Another story about the awareness of animals came from Nora, a scientist doing research on cancer. Nora saw me for anxiety. One of the issues that caused her emotional turmoil was that she liked research, but her experiments required killing the rabbits who were her research subjects. I was aware that Native Americans apologize to the animals they kill for meat. I suggested to Nora that she apologize to the animals she worked with, and thank them for giving up their lives for her research.

In our next session Nora was upbeat. She said that she talked with her rabbits before each experiment. She apologized to them, told the rabbits the research was important, and she thanked them. She was amazed that after she included this step, she began getting almost twice the amount of serum per rabbit than she got before she included the apology and thanking them.

The following animal story involves a different species. It was told by Liam, a budget analyst employed by the federal government in Washington, D.C. His hobby is wildlife photography, and this event took place at a National Wildlife Refuge on one of the barrier islands off the Atlantic coast.

Wild Swans

I went out early because I get my best pictures around sunrise and sunset. I was walking along the freshwater lagoon as the sun came over the horizon. The scene was stunning: golden light glistened off the water, and two magnificent swans were backlit by the rising sun. They were a good distance away, but I was so moved I quietly said, "You're beautiful. I'm glad you're here, and I'm glad I'm here to see you."

Then I heard a voice. I knew it was inside my head, but it said, "We'd like to show you something." Then both swans changed their direction and began swimming toward each other at a ninety-degree angle. When they were nearing the point where they would converge, an otter popped up in the water.

Animals are sentient beings, and they have awareness. They can communicate over distance—in Liam's example, from about 100 yards away, but in Sheldrake's example, 80 miles. Liam's experience is unusual in that words were used. In general, animals have a limited verbal vocabulary and rarely understand more than 50 words, but they are sensitive to many nuances in body language. For example, in most of the stories I hear about ESP between humans and animals, the animals are dogs. In those ESP stories between humans and dogs, the thinking is usually in visual images.

It should be pointed out that I do not believe that Liam had a hallucination. I had worked with Liam on his high anxiety level and some other issues, but he was in relatively good shape from a mental health standpoint, and I am certain he is not psychotic.

Experiences like Liam's are common among Native Americans. Stanley Krippner told about an unfortunate Native American woman who went for a medical checkup and was asked by a newly trained psychiatrist whether she heard voices. She replied that she heard voices all the time. It was part of her spiritual tradition to hear the voices of nature, but the poor woman was put in the psychiatric ward. She was also given anti-psychotic medication, which she pretended to swallow but discarded later. Fortunately the problem was resolved within a short time.

One of the more unusual stories I have heard about animals came from Fred, a personal friend. He loved his dog for many years until she died of cancer and other age-related diseases. A few years after the dog's death, Fred told me that he sometimes had a feeling her spirit was with him. He had heard of Susan Knilans, a psychic who could contact the spirits of deceased animals. Hearing that, I became skeptical and told Fred to be careful about getting scammed. Fred said that the cost was modest, and he thought it was worth a chance. He went ahead and made an appointment.

He was delighted with the results. The psychic told him several things that astonished him. The psychic said that the dog often was with him in spirit, and she liked traveling with him. Fred had recently taken a job that required several overseas trips each year. The psychic also said that the dog liked the cat. Fred's wife had gotten a cat as a pet. The final item the psychic reported was seeing a blue triangle. One of his dog's favorite toys was a blue rubber triangle that they used for playing tug of war. What is the probability that Susan Knilans could have made these three hits by chance?

Modern pharmacologists have been puzzled by the ability of Native Americans to find medicinal herbs and plants that are clinically effective. Indigenous people of South America used bark containing quinine to treat malaria, and in the U.S. west a plant containing ephedrine was used for asthma. Sometimes medicines of indigenous people were co-opted; for example, Native Americans used a willow bark tea for fevers and aches. The bark contains salicylic acid. Adolph Bayer added an acetyl group to the molecule, and acetylsalicylic acid, or aspirin, was born. V.J. Vogel has found that over 170 remedies which have been or are in the *Pharmacopeia of the United States* were used by Native Americans in the U.S., and more remedies were used by tribes south of the border. Native Americans did not use double-blind research techniques or controlled clinical trials for discovering medicinal plants. How did they discover the remedies?

Several years ago in the Smokey Mountains along the North Carolina – Tennessee border I met Tom, one of the few remaining Eastern Band Cherokee medicine men. He had a small shop where I bought some herbs for a sinus problem. There were no other customers, and we talked for a couple of hours. I asked him how his people learned which plants are effective for which illnesses. He said that once a particular plant was found to be a remedy, this knowledge was passed down from older medicine people to younger ones in an apprentice-like manner.

To learn which plant was useful in the first place, a medicine person would go out into the wilderness after some fasting and prayer, quiet the mind, and talk to the plants. The plants would reveal their particular healing abilities. Tom said it was important to ask permission when harvesting plants. With a quiet mind, one silently asks which of a particular group of the same plants volunteered themselves to be picked and used. Tom said that whichever plants draw one's attention at that time could be picked.

There was a note of sadness and concern in Tom's voice. He said that he was worried he was growing old and none of the Cherokee young men in the area were interested in becoming medicine men. He was concerned that he might not be able to pass on his knowledge before he died. I have tried to locate him since then, but without success. He was an older man when we met, and I suspect he has died.

Our relationship to animals and plants is mysterious and complex. We are more connected than we realize. I do not believe that this means that we should necessarily become vegetarians. Many deeply spiritual people are meat eaters; for example, the Tibetans and also the Native Americans. I know Native American men who hunt, but they offer prayers to the spirits of the animals they kill, and thank them for giving their bodies to provide people with energy and vitality.

One Native American friend, a retired teacher, keeps a cooler with meat cutting tools in the trunk of his car. He knows how to judge meat, and when he sees a road-killed deer, he stops and checks for freshness. If the meat is still good, he harvests it and takes it away in the cooler. He said that he sometimes gets as much as fifty pounds of meat from a large deer. After putting it in his home freezer, he burns herbs and offers prayers in honor of the dead animal.

Chapter Twelve

Assorted Mysteries and Anomalies

The Possibility of Other Dimensions

Electrons and even the nuclei of atoms can disappear and reappear later. Where do they go when they disappear? Some physicists suggest that they may go into another dimension. This raises the question of whether other dimensions exist, and if so, how many dimensions are there?

When I heard the next story I believed it was an example of a ghost. When I discussed it with a friend who is studying the Kabbalah, he suggested a different explanation. The Kabbalah is a mystical tradition within Judaism, but one need not be Jewish to find wisdom in the Kabbalah. In many respects it is a technology rather than a dogma. The use of a particular procedure yields a particular result. Many Kabbalahist teachings are conveyed through stories, and an interesting story involves other dimensions.

In the story, a wealthy man and his wife were unable to have children. The man consulted a wise Kabbalahist to learn what prevented him and his wife from conceiving. He was told he had to obtain forgiveness from a woman he had wronged in his youth. If he could obtain her forgiveness, his wife would conceive. After a long and difficult search, he finally found the woman and asked for forgiveness. She said that there was a young couple in her family who wished to marry but could not afford a wedding. She said that she would forgive the man on the condition that he arrange a fine wedding and pay for it. He hosted and paid for a great wedding.

In time, the man's own wife conceived. When he told a relative of the woman that she had forgiven him, the astounded relative told him that it was not possible. The woman had died shortly after he abandoned her. This is the Kabbalah way of teaching that a person can exist in several dimensions, and in Kabbalah it is believed that a person might have parallel lives in as many as ten dimensions. Similar beliefs exist in the folklore of other countries; one of the best known is the *doppelganger* in Germany.

The following story from an inmate suggests the possibility of a parallel life in another dimension, or that he saw a ghost.

The Beard and Tattoo

My father was a good guy when I was little, but when I was about eight he got into drugs. My mom started fighting with him over that, and finally they got a divorce. After they were divorced about a year, he had a heart attack and died. I know he died because I saw his body at the wake and I went to the burial.

A couple of years later I was in the car with my mom when we were driving through Baltimore. We stopped for a light, and I saw a guy standing on the corner staring at us. It was my father. He had the same beard and tattoo, but I knew my father had died. I said, "Hey Mom, look at him," and I pointed. She looked and she started to cry. Then the light changed, cars behind us started honking, and she drove away.

The inmate who told this story did it with a lot of emotion, and he sounded bewildered. I believe that he had experienced what he reported. I should remind the reader that this and all other stories in this book have been included only when there were emotional responses congruent with the material reported.

I do not know whether the inmate saw a ghost or if he experienced a double. The question of whether he thought he had a double was put to Robert A. Monroe, a former radio and TV executive who authored *Journeys Out of the Body*. Monroe replied that he thought he had one, and said that he was given a name and address on one of his journeys. Monroe admitted that as of that time he had not found the courage to contact the man.

Little People

The popular movie *What the Bleep Do We Know?* is an entertaining introduction to quantum physics. In the movie the protagonist, Amanda (Marlee Matlin), is asked, "How far down the rabbit hole do you want to go?" In other words, how far does she want to go looking at common assumptions, because we can get answers that are strange and bewildering.

Modern Americans assume that tales of little people are limited to, for instance, Irish or Norse folklore, that they are only fantasy and not to be taken seriously. Yet many cultures have a firm belief in little people, especially in the northern Germanic and Celtic countries. The Inuit believe in little people. Hawaiians believe in the Menhune, a little people who inhabited the islands before the ancestors of the current Polynesians arrived. The belief is strong among the indigenous peoples of North America. The Cherokee, Shoshoni, Arapahoe, Choctaw, Crow, and Muskogee-Creek all have extensive tales in which the little people can be mischievous or helpful, especially to medicine men and medicine women.

David Lewis, Jr., a full-blooded Muskogee-Creek and practicing medicine man, has told of a little person who helped him. Lewis first met the little man when he was seven years old. This was shortly after his father and grandmother, who were both medicine people, began initiating Lewis into the medicine way. One day he was fishing on a flat rock by a stream, his favorite spot, when he saw a little man standing on a fallen tree. To be sure he was not dreaming, Lewis stood up. The little man said, "I'll be with you till the day you die."

Lewis was sure the creature was always present, but the man was only visible occasionally. He became visible when needed. For example, the man would show Lewis a plant he had difficulty finding that was necessary to prepare a remedy for someone. The man would point to a plant and say, "Over there, that's what you need." Lewis noted that the man did not seem to age over the years. I was curious about why the man was only visible some of the time, and how he controlled when he appeared.

It should be noted that Lewis is clear-headed. He has worked extensively with the anthropologist Ann Jordan, and together they've published a collaborative book documenting Muskogee-Creek medicine ways. Jordan holds the medicine man in high regard.

Iceland presents a puzzle when it comes to little people, because the level of education is high and the country technologically advanced. Many of the buildings are heated with geothermal energy, and it is the only county where I have seen a gas station that also dispenses hydrogen for hydrogen-powered cars. Yet a substantial percentage of the population believes in gnomes, trolls and elves. In surveys more than half of those questioned said they have seen little people. Highway engineers design roads to go around rather than through places where those creatures are said to live. The engineers do not necessarily admit to believing in the little people, but say that if they avoid those areas with homes of "hidden folk," there are fewer injuries among workers and less equipment breakdowns.

On a vacation in Iceland my wife, Nancy, and I stayed for a week on the Snaefellsness Peninsula, which extends like a muscular arm sixty miles into the North Atlantic from the northwest coast of Iceland. The entire peninsula has been shrouded in mystical lore from pagan Viking days to the present. In *The Journey to the Center of the Earth* Jules Verne used the Snaefellsjokull glacier as the starting point for his fictional team of scientists to explore the interior of the planet. At Hellnar, a statue of Mary stands over a spring where Catholics believe an apparition occurred in the early 1200s.

MYSTICAL EXPERIENCES

New-Agers believe that the peninsula contains intersecting ley lines, as well as a strong energy vortex or power spot. Ley lines are alignments along the earth's surface that are considered to resonate a mystical or psychic energy. Some believe that ancient monuments and megaliths were constructed along ley lines.

Having brought crampons and trekking poles, we intended to hike across the glacier, but Gudrun, an attractive blond widow and owner of the Hellnar Hotel, warned us not to go. It was September and Gudrun said that the summer sun had weakened the ice, creating hidden crevasses. We would be in danger of disappearing into the glacier. Late spring, she added, is the time to hike the glacier.

After her warning, which might very well have saved us, we became friendly with Gudrun. I asked her about the seeming contradiction between the intellectual sophistication of Icelanders and the belief in elves, gnomes and trolls. She insisted that those creatures do exist, but maintained they are in another dimension. Either a naturally occurring trance or a shamanic journey is necessary to perceive them.

Since I had learned to make shamanic journeys with a drum beat at a particular frequency from Michael Harner, I asked about caves in the area suitable for making a journey. Gudrun recommended Songhellir cave, on the side of the extinct volcano that supported the glacier. She told us that Songhellir was used over 1,000 years ago for shamanic rituals by Bradur, a chieftain who had great strength and shamanic powers. Bradur descended from a line of Sami (Laplander) shamans and was reputed to be able to predict the future.

We reached Songhellir through a combination of driving and hiking. In the cave, after our eyes adjusted to the darkness, we found comfortable places. Then Nancy and I took turns drumming for each other. Remarkable things can be done with a drum. Michael Harner has joked that if the FDA knew what could be done with a drum, they would try to classify it as a controlled, dangerous substance. At Songhellir cave we used a large but shallow drum with a single skin, similar to those used by Irish musicians.

When Nancy drummed for me, my journey took me to a lower stratum, where I encountered creatures from Icelandic folklore. A group of elfin men wearing trousers and boots but no shirts were working hard and soaked in sweat. At first they appeared to be mining, but closer inspection showed that they were repairing a local fault line in the earth. A projection of rock had stopped movement along the fault, causing dangerous tensions to build. If movement was not restored, a local earthquake could result.

As I moved to get a closer view, a fully clothed elfin man, who appeared to be the foreman, stepped in front of me. He appeared older than the workers and he had a gray beard. He blocked my path and said important work was taking place. I was not to intrude or cause delays. Shortly afterwards Nancy gave the drumming signal for me to make the return journey and come out of the trance.

Never again will I smirk when someone talks about little people or hidden folk. My respect for Icelanders likewise has increased. Like the rest of the planet, they struggled with the financial meltdown of 2008, but they are able to keep a foot in both worlds. They have been able to integrate their belief in elves and similar creatures, while at the same time creating a technically advanced, modern society.

Psychic Knowledge of Death and Supernatural Warnings

Several patients have told me that they learned of the death of a relative or spouse through a dream. Martha, a college student, was home with her family for the summer when she had an unusual dream. In her dream she saw her grandmother's room, which was filled with golden light, with several relatives and close friends gathered around the bed. Martha and her grandmother were close. They had a special relationship, and Martha understood the meaning of her dream.

MYSTICAL EXPERIENCES

When she went downstairs for breakfast in the morning, she told her parents, "Granny died last night." Her parents were startled, because Granny was elderly and frail, but she had not been ill. Shortly afterward the family received a phone call telling them of Granny's death. Martha's dad had taken the call, and he asked who was there in Granny's room. The people present matched those Martha had seen in her dream. Martha believes that the dream was Granny's way of saying "Goodbye."

An inmate had a similar dream. He was close to his grandmother; many inmates from the inner cities are closer to grandparents than to their parents. He had a dream in which his grandmother visited him in jail, and it left him with a strange feeling when he woke in the morning. When he requested a phone call to his family, he learned his grandmother had died during the night. This African-American inmate from the inner city had a similar experience to the middle-class young woman from an affluent family. On the spiritual level, we are all very much alike.

Another woman, Lorrie, had a similar dream about her mother. At the time Lorrie's mother was elderly and sick. Lorrie dreamed that she was with her mother helping her pack for a trip, and a bridal gown was among the things they were packing. In the morning Lorrie learned that her mother had died during the night. Lorrie has studied symbolism in myths. She realized that packing for a trip was a symbol for going somewhere, and that a bridal gown is a symbol for a major life change for a person. When people marry, they go from one stage of life to another.

Premonitions and supernatural warnings are similar to receiving psychic awareness of death. Many of the inmates who have been wounded in gun fights before their incarceration have told me they had a hunch or premonition before they were shot. Army veterans have told me that when they saw a squad about to go out on a mission, they knew which men would not be coming back.

The most unusual story of premonitions came from an elderly veteran. Hans was a professional soldier most of his adult life. Born in Central Europe, he was conscripted into the German army when he was in his late teens and sent to the Russian front. One evening he had a dream in which he looked at himself in the mirror, and his left shoulder was missing in his reflection. In battle the next day he was wounded in that shoulder.

He was sent back for treatment, but when he recuperated Hans was sent to North Africa. The same thing happened. In a dream there was no reflection from one leg in the mirror, and the following day Hans was wounded in that leg. Once again he was sent for treatment, but when he recovered, he was sent to France to fight against the Allies shortly after the Normandy invasion. The same thing happened in France.

After World War II, Hans was impressed by the American soldiers who had occupied the area where he lived. There were no local jobs, so Hans got a job working at the American base. During that time he decided to immigrate to America and become a U.S. citizen. Then, as now, enlisting in the U.S. armed forces made the path to citizenship easier. Hans went to a recruiting center, joined and spent the rest of his career in the Army. He fought in Korea and Vietnam and was decorated for his actions in both wars. While in the U.S. Army, Hans was wounded four more times, bringing his total number of combat wounds to seven. Each time Hans was wounded, the evening before he had a dream in which there was no reflection in the mirror of the area that would be wounded.

Although Hans' premonitions were about being wounded, many people, including President Lincoln, had warnings prior to their deaths. About ten days before he was shot, Lincoln dreamed that he heard a great deal of sobbing. In the dream he followed the sobbing to the East Room, where he saw several people and soldiers guarding a corpse wrapped in funeral vestments. Lincoln asked a soldier, "Who is dead in the White House?" The soldier answered, "The President. He was killed by an assassin." Lincoln said that he was disturbed by the dream and he could not get back to sleep that night. He also indicated that the dream continued to bother him for days afterward.

The Irish legend of the banshee is a well-known warning about forthcoming death. The banshee is a spirit, usually described as female, who alerts families by wailing, warning them that one of their members will soon die. The banshee never reveals who will die, but they reveal that death is coming. Although many are terrified by the banshee's wail, the intent is actually benevolent. It enables the family to coalesce and prepare for the coming emotional blow.

The word "banshee" is usually translated as "a female spirit from the mounds." Prehistoric man-made mounds dot the Irish landscape. In folklore they are considered the gateway to the lower world. This is similar to the gateways to the lower world in shamanic cultures. In Irish mythology the mounds are also considered to be the homes of fairies, and the homes of the prehistoric peoples who lived in Ireland. The myths say that the earlier inhabitants retreated to the lower world after they were conquered by the Celtic people, who are the ancestors of the modern Irish.

The mounds were sacred for traditional Irish. Ned, an older man I talked with in County Kildare, told me a story from his childhood during lambing time. On his father's farm, it was Ned's job to help the ewes when one had difficulty giving birth. Sometimes a ewe having a problem would wander into a mound at night. Ned had to go in and help, but being in the mound at night terrified him and he dreaded that task.

Henry Glassie, a professor at the University of Pennsylvania, told an interesting story about a mound when he visited a farm in Ireland with his friend, Joe. The woman who owned the farm, a relative of Joe, took them into a mound on her property. A branch from a bush crossed their path when they went into the mound, and Joe broke it off. This upset the woman and she said, "No good will come from Joe's breaking a branch in the mound."

This occurred in the late 1970s, before digital pictures replaced film. Joe had a roll of film for 36 pictures in his camera. He snapped pictures from 22 through 28 in the mound and the remainder later. When Joe got home and had the film developed, pictures one through 21 and from 29 to 36 came out fine. Shots 22 to 28 were totally blank.

Unfortunately, Ireland is losing some of its traditions. In the evening many young people stay at home surfing the Internet rather than visiting the local pub to commune with neighbors. Agriculture is becoming more intensive. Some farmers are clearing the brush and sowing crops on the ancient mounds on their land. In prior generations the mounds were not disturbed. On my most recent visit to Ireland there was a heated debate about a plan to build the M3, a highway which would have infringed upon the sacred hill of Tara and the surrounding mounds. This would have been unthinkable a generation ago.

Despite these changes, people still tell of encounters with banshees, but less often than those I heard in an Irish-American community in my youth. Some occur in America, which is interesting because the traditional belief is that a banshee was attached to particular extended families. This would suggest that banshees accompanied some of the families that came to the new world.

Declan, an Irish-American, told me this story. He was born in the U.S., but his family was from Ireland. At the time of the story he was eight or nine and visiting his grandparents' home with his sister in a rural part of New Jersey. One afternoon his grandfather was in the hospital with what was thought to be a minor illness, and his sister was shopping with their grandmother. Declan was alone in the house, and he decided to explore the place.

He had been in the unfinished attic before; it was used as a storage area by the family, so it had many things interesting to a young boy. On the way up the attic steps, Declan heard wailing from above. He knew he was the only one in the house, and he was so scared he ran outside, staying there until his grandmother and sister returned. His grandfather died two days later.

A woman in the central part of Ireland told me a story of a banshee, but the person who died had immigrated to America. Her father, Bill, had inherited the family farm, but his younger brother James decided to immigrate to America because small farms could not be subdivided. James had been interested in flying since he was a boy, so after he arrived in America he enlisted in the U.S. Air Force. Eventually James was stationed at a base in Texas and was doing well. Two years later Bill heard loud wailing during the night, and his first thought was that cats were fighting. He talked to neighbors the next day, and none of the homes in the neighborhood had cats, and no one had seen cats in the area. The telegram arrived that evening. James had been killed in a plane crash in Texas.

Reports of Extraterrestrial Contact, UFOs and Abductions

There has only been one sign of extraterrestrial life that is widely accepted. In August 1977 a radio signal from outer space was received at the Ohio State Radio Observatory in Delaware County, Ohio. At that time Ohio State University had a huge facility with an antenna grid the size of three football fields, and that picked up the signal. This signal is often called the "Wow" signal because the scientist on duty at the time, Dr. Jerry Ehman, wrote "Wow" in the margin of the computer printout.

The Ohio State facility has since been dismantled, but the SETI (Search for Extraterrestrial Intelligence) Institute has more sophisticated electronic telescope arrays at various locations. Their site in Northern California has 42 antennas, but no signals have been picked up thus far. Part of the problem is the huge distances in space, usually measured in light years. A signal from a planet in a distant galaxy might take a century or more to reach Earth.

The reports of UFO sightings are far more controversial than the 1977 radio signal. Are UFOs real, the work of pranksters, or are they simply natural phenomena, such as weather balloons? If real, where do they come from? Despite the amount of light pollution in our night skies, why are they not seen by more people? Jacques Vallee has raised some interesting hypotheses. He speculates that UFOs may be from another dimension, and switch back and forth from another dimension into ours.

Reports of UFOs are not new. Clonmacnoise, on the River Shannon, was one of the two largest monasteries in medieval Ireland. A manuscript written in the 1300s said that a ship in the air appeared over the monks. A man came down from the ship, "swimming in the air," but he appeared to have trouble breathing and went back to the ship.

In the 1970s I saw a UFO in the southeastern U.S. from a plane as we flew across the Chattahoochee River, crossing from Alabama into Georgia. The pilot casually said, "Look up on the left, there's one of those things we've been reading about in the papers." All six of us on board saw a slightly oblong shiny object, stationary for a few moments, and then it quickly moved away. There were military bases in the area, including Eglin Air Force Base and Pensacola Naval Air Station in northwest Florida, and an Army helicopter flight school at Ft. Rucker, Alabama. It could have been a military aircraft, but it did not look like any that I was familiar with, although it could have been a secret prototype from Area 51 in Nevada.

Since then several patients have told me of UFO sightings. This following case was clinically important because of the distress the patient felt over it. He was an African-American young man from a rural area of Maryland.

Watchin'

One summer night when I was about ten, it had just gotten dark and I was wrestling with my brother in the back yard. All of a

MYSTICAL EXPERIENCES

sudden this ball shaped thing was up above us. It was bigger than this room, and bluish fire was comin' off it. It stayed there for a few minutes, then took off. We both saw it and my brother said, "Damn! What was that?" Ever since then it feels like someone is watchin' me.

This patient was not paranoid. He did not have traits common to a paranoid personality, but he did have a high anxiety level, and that was the focus of his treatment. I do not know how much of his anxiety was due to the UFO experience, or how much that experience exacerbated a pre-existing condition.

Larry, an electronics technician and level-headed guy, told me of a UFO experience while on an elk hunting trip in the U.S. west. An experienced hunter he knew told him the best time is before sunrise, so Larry went out early while it was still dark. As he was looking for elk, he came up over a rise and noticed a bright light shining down on the ground from about one hundred feet in the air. The light was as bright as daylight and made no sound at all. As it advanced toward him, Larry became scared and ran. Now he says he wishes he had stayed to find out more.

The topic gets more attention in the press out west, perhaps because the population is less dense and therefore there is less light pollution. As recently as June 2010 the Santa Fe newspaper, *The New Mexican*, ran an article on the topic with a photo of a pasture circle reportedly made by a UFO landing.

I have dealt with one case of abduction. A physician friend referred one of his patients to me for an in-depth psychological testing and evaluation. The patient told him that he had been abducted and subjected to medical tests on a UFO. The patient was a sixty-year-old veteran with an IQ higher than average. He was well oriented and presented no confusion or any signs of psychosis. From a mental health viewpoint, he did not have signs of a disorder that required treatment. He was an average man, and he was not seeking attention, for he told only three or four people about his experience.

An interesting case involves Paul Laffoley, an artist whose work is on display at the American Visionary Art Museum in Baltimore. Laffoley claims that he has been abducted and a device implanted in his brain. People who heard his claim dismissed him as delusional, but when brain images were taken in a medical examination, a metallic object was found near the base of his brain. It was not removed because that would have required risky brain surgery, and doctors considered it better to leave the object in place. This case is important because physical evidence was found in Laffoley's brain.

John Mack, a former professor of psychiatry at Harvard Medical School, was the most knowledgeable person on abduction. At first Mack was skeptical about both UFOs and reports of abduction, but he changed his position after seeing several patients. Eventually he worked intensively with two hundred people who said that they had been abducted. He was impressed with the consistency of the stories, the sincerity of the people, and the emotions expressed as they gave their accounts.

Mack also noted physical evidence on their bodies, such as skin ulcerations, cuts, and triangle-shaped lesions that were consistent with the patients' reports. Male abductees had said samples of their sperm were collected, and females said eggs were removed. This has caused some to speculate that the aliens may be trying to develop a backup for preserving the human race in case we destroy ourselves through nuclear war or poison our planet. Mack hypnotized a number of his patients and found their reports did not vary whether or not they were hypnotized.

Mack showed great intellectual courage in following the clinical evidence he encountered and writing about it in the open literature. Although his credentials as a psychiatrist were impeccable, and earlier his biography of T.E. Lawrence had earned a Pulitzer Prize,

MYSTICAL EXPERIENCES

Harvard almost fired him. The university appointed a committee to evaluate Mack, but after fifteen months of meetings and discussion it declined to take action. Despite the fine words about intellectual freedom in American universities, investigating topics that embarrass institutions can damage a professor's career.

The scientist and former astronaut Edgar Mitchell startled many when he was interviewed on a British radio station on July 23, 2008. Mitchell said that a UFO had crashed near Roswell, New Mexico in 1947. Several writers had made this claim earlier, but Mitchell's comments were more credible. He is a competent scientist and former astronaut who grew up in the Roswell area. He was a senior in high school at the time of the crash. Mitchell knew many of the local people, and they insist the crash was real.

Several residents of the Roswell area have said that they are disclosing the details of the 1947 crash because they are now elderly and want the information to come out before they go to their graves. Among the details locals have disclosed is that there were four alien bodies from the crash; three were dead and one was still alive. They were described as small, about the size of a ten-year-old child, but with large heads. The sand in the area of the crash was crystallized, which would have required intense heat. Material from the crash included small metal I-beams and a thin metallic material that had "memory"; if bent, twisted or even beaten with a hammer, it would return to its original shape. Locals also said that planes came in from Wright Field in Ohio to take debris away.

Residents who were involved with the crash site reported that they were told not to talk about it, and a few received heavy-handed threats. Some were told that if they talked, something bad would happen, not only to them but also to their families. A local radio station that broadcast the story was warned they could lose their license.

In addition to the threats, there has been a continuing campaign of disinformation. The Air Force has claimed the crash debris was a weather balloon. There have also been claims that UFO sightings are only flares released by military pilots in training, since flares are a counter-measure against heat-seeking missiles.

Why would the U.S. government threaten its citizens and engage in disinformation? There are two possibilities. The first is that they are concerned the public could not handle knowing the truth, and widespread panic would follow. That assumption is based on a radio program aired on October 30, 1938. The actor and movie director Orson Welles modified the British novel *War of the Worlds* by H.G. Wells (no relation) and had it re-written as a radio play. He set the story in the U.S. rather than England. In the play Martians attacked New York and New Jersey. Many listeners tuned in late, missed the introduction, and thought it was a news bulletin rather than fiction. There was some panic, but historians say that the reports of panic at that time were exaggerated. Most listeners briefly tuned into other stations and realized they were listening to fiction.

The second reason for the threats to witnesses and the spread of disinformation involves military secrecy. Some say that back engineering has been used on the recovered UFO material to improve U.S. military aircraft. Those who hold this view say that lessons learned from the crashed UFO in Roswell have already been incorporated into the design of military aircraft. An example is the flexible skin of the F-22, which makes it more difficult to detect on radar.

Mitchell has said that there is no reason to fear the UFOs. As he has pointed out, their technology is far more advanced than ours, and if they had harmful intentions, they could have carried them out long ago. It also appears that more disclosure by various governments is on the way, and acceptance will occur. On Native American reservations medicine people and tribal elders have had enough contact that they believe in aliens and call them "star people." High-level officials in the Brazilian Air Force have begun disclosing previously secret reports of encounters between their planes and UFOs. Britain recently disclosed that Churchill ordered sightings of UFOs kept secret.

My colleague, Victoria, has another hypothesis to account for the lack of acceptance of UFOs, ESP and paranormal phenomena in general. She believes that male competitiveness is the reason. She says men fear being considered less tough-minded and less macho than other guys if they admit to believing in the paranormal.

Chapter Thirteen

Making Changes for Emotional Growth

The Brazilian writer Paulo Coelho's novel *The Alchemist* has been translated into 67 languages and has sold more than 30 million copies. The novel is a brilliant allegory about a poor shepherd boy from the south of Spain who eventually finds a rich, fulfilling life. The central theme in Coelho's work is that anyone can change his or her life. The *Financial Times* writer A.N. Wilson, however, has said that Coelho's idea is fundamentally false and that people are trapped by circumstances.

It is not that change is impossible, but that there is enormous resistance to change. Often the change is precipitated by outside events, like the loss of a job or a divorce. People are reluctant to change and find it difficult. Many patients entering psychotherapy are seeking ways to suffer more bravely rather than making the changes that will enable them to avoid suffering.

Spiritual teachers in India say that this wish to avoid changing is an ego preservation mechanism. But like the towns in Western movies where the buildings are fakes with only a propped-up front, the ego is also a false front. It is not the core of our being. To advance in spiritual knowledge and wisdom, the ego must be conquered. As Goethe put it, "He who does not conquer himself remains always a slave."

Because of resistance to change, direct advice almost never works. People respond with the "Yes, but..." game. My patients usually find it easier to make changes for emotional growth if I tell a story, give a concrete example from another case, or quote advice from someone else. Since hope is important in psychotherapy, and patients with spiritual beliefs are more hopeful, I encourage spiritual practices, but this has to be done with care. I do not recommend any particular religion. When working with a young man who is drifting, unemployed or underemployed, I tell him I am not a Freudian, but nevertheless the old man had some wisdom. Then I tell him Freud's famous line about the two things a man should do: "*Lieben und Arbeiten*," or love and work.

When a patient tries to duck the painful introspection necessary for successful psychotherapy and expects too much direction, I often tell the story of Milton Erickson and the horse. When Erickson was a boy in the early 1900s, a valuable horse wandered into his yard. Young Milton got on the horse, which had a bridle, and directed it out to the road. On the road Milton slacked up on the reins, and the horse started going down the road. If the horse stopped to eat some grass or drink from a stream, Milton allowed it briefly, then led the horse back to the road. On the road he again slacked up on the reins.

After a couple of hours they reached a farmhouse, and the horse went into the yard and stood there. Milton tied the reins to a fence post and knocked on the door. A farmer came out, saw the horse and thanked Milton for returning it. But then the farmer asked with a puzzled look, "How did you know where I live? How did you know where to bring the horse?" Milton replied, "I didn't. I just kept him on the road, and he found his own way home." Then I tell the patient, "That is how psychotherapy works."

This might seem odd to those who put a high value on intellectual understanding, but stories sometimes work better when the patient does not get the point or see the connection. It can be good when they are left wondering, "What the hell did he mean by that?" It is difficult for them to maintain resistance when their mind is exploring different possibilities and searching for an answer that fits.

MYSTICAL EXPERIENCES

I used this technique, along with some other procedures, on a woman patient who had emotional issues with her parents as well as a phobia about driving across high bridges. She worked on the issues and forgave her parents for mistakes they had made. Although her elderly parents lived in a nearby state, she had not visited them in several years because the trip would have involved driving across two high bridges. At her next session she joyfully announced, "I visited my parents over the weekend." She did not see the connection between the previous session and her achievement.

The use of stories to help people grow emotionally did not begin in the twentieth century with modern psychotherapy. Some fairy tales and children's stories have this function. *The Wizard of Oz* and *Little Red Riding Hood* are examples. *Little Red Riding Hood* is good way of telling children that people may not be what they seem. The world's great myths are also teaching tales that have been used for thousands of years in most cultures around the globe. These mythic stories range from Homer's *Odyssey*, written about 800 BC, to George Lucas' *Star Wars*. The myths appear in Africa, Asia, Oceania, Mesoamerica, and almost all the cultures of Europe.

Joseph Campbell analyzed these myths, which he published in *The Hero with a Thousand Faces*. Campbell found three major phases of the myths, with five to six steps within each of these. In the myths the hero or the heroine receives a call to go on an adventure, but he or she initially reject the call; in other words, the person does not want to change. The hero or heroine usually follows the call after receiving spiritual or supernatural help. The heroic figure goes through trials and temptations before achieving the quest. Eventually the hero must return to his/her home, but as a changed man or woman. A sample of the myths that fit Campbell's model and also foster emotional maturity are:

Myth	Cultural Origin
Gilgamesh	Babylonia
Osiris	Egypt
Odyssey	Greece
Ramayana	India
Lion King	Mali
Popul Vuh	Quiche' Mayan
Quetzacoatl	Pre-Columban Mexico
Tain bo Cuailnge	Pre-Christian Ireland
Beowulf	Anglo-Saxon
Nibelungenlied	German
The Sagas	Iceland
Kalevala	Finland
Kotan Utunnai	Ainu of Japan
Watunna	Yekuana of Venezuela

These myths are entertaining, but they are not mere entertainment. They present role models and instructions for the young. In some cultures these myths have taken on the quality of a sacred text. Although the myths were memorized in ancient times, when much of the population was not literate, in India many people continue to memorize and recite *The Ramayana*. With 24,000 couplets, this is no small achievement.

Ancient people knew the importance of these myths. Several of them, for example the *Tain bo Cuailnge* and the *Ramayana*, contain blessings for those who memorize them. Modern writers continue to borrow from the ancient myths. The *Lord of the Rings* lifts material from the *Nibelungen*, Hogwarts Academy in the Harry Potter tales resembles the old Welsh and Irish bardic schools, and Hollywood borrowed an African story for the *Lion King* movie.

Campbell's analysis of myths is a scholarly masterpiece, but the emotional and maturational messages within the myths have more

MYSTICAL EXPERIENCES

interest for me than the structure. Myths can be seen as parables that contain lessons. Some of the lessons in myth are:

- We must go on a journey, or in other words, change from an earlier way of living.
- Often spiritual or magical help is needed.
- There are dark and dangerous times when we need courage and persistence.
- We must resist temptation and be loyal. Odysseus was not distracted by the temptations of Circe from his goal of saving his men.
- When we do not have enough power to overcome our adversaries, we must rely on cleverness and creativity. Odysseus disguised himself as a beggar to overcome Penelope's suitors.
- Eventually we return home, where we must blend our new changes into our lives.

The lives of some of my patients fit several of Campbell's steps. One patient, Gene, did not want to change. He did not come in for counseling voluntarily, but rather at his probation officer's insistence. At first Gene resisted the process; then he engaged and became an active participant. He was a young man in his mid twenties. Although it was a blue-collar job, he made good money as a skilled welder. Gene had three or four friends that he hung out with on weekend evenings. Their idea of a good time was to go bar hopping, "catch a buzz," try to pick up girls, and occasionally get into a fight. In warm weather there was a little variation; they would drive around drinking with the windows open and holler at the pretty girls.

Gene met Linda and they began dating. He and Linda moved in together, and gradually he saw less of his friends. He had been living with Linda for about a year when Gene got antsy and nostalgic for his old buddies. He told Linda that on Friday night he was going out with his friends. She was not happy about it, but on Friday night he went out. His buddies were glad to see him, and they went carousing as usual. They were talking to some girls in a bar, and one was coming on to Gene. Gene thought she was phony, wore too much make-up, and laughed too loud. He was not having fun, and he asked himself, "What the hell am I doing here?" Gene excused himself and went home to Linda. The last time I saw him they were planning to get married.

On that Friday night Gene and his friends did the same things they had done in earlier years, but Gene had changed and those activities were no longer fun. He had moved on to a more mature level. Carousing was less satisfying than the intimacy and companionship he found with Linda. I find this case interesting because it illustrates the process of change. No amount of lecturing or haranguing would have dissuaded Gene from going out with his friends. He had to re-experience his older way of doing things to know that it felt empty compared to his more fulfilling life with Linda.

Something analogous happens with spirituality. Often no number of words can convince us to make changes; we need to have an experience. With me, it was Blanche seeing me working in an office two years before it happened. That led me to question some of my assumptions about the material world, and I became more interested in spirituality. A person who does not believe that we often get help from a spiritual source might need to have an experience like the African-American young man who heard a voice utter "Get outta the car" seconds before the car was destroyed.

A number of practices are conducive to one's having a spiritual experience. An Indian holy man, Sri Siva, believes that making changes is easier if we make a spiritual change first. He uses the analogy of the forms of water. It is difficult to move a glacier in the mountains, and liquid water can be channeled with effort, but it is easier to control and move steam. Sri Siva says that to make lasting changes, it is easiest if we begin with the spiritual level, and then move to the mental, and finally to the physical body. To take an example, his students with weight problems say they were far more successful with losing weight and keeping it off when they followed these steps.

Some clergy in mainstream denominations believe that alternative spiritual practices are a threat to their religion. I do not understand this attitude. The threat to traditional religion is not the revival of Wicca or shamanism, but a belief that the whole realm of spirituality is a delusion, that only the material exists. A visit to Europe shows the decline in spiritual beliefs. The churches are almost empty on Sundays. Even in Spain, where the culture of Catholicism runs deep, only elderly people attend Sunday Mass. Many people have dropped their beliefs in religion, God, or spiritual beings.

On the other hand, some small groups continue to have strong spiritual beliefs. I have had several Wiccan patients over the years who are deeply spiritual and appreciate the value of ritual. Similarly, those who practice shamanism do not have to be convinced that there is a soul or spirit that survives the death of the physical body. They know it. They have encountered the dead on shamanic journeys.

Part V:

Techniques to Experience Spiritual Wisdom

The particular practices described here are included because I have experienced them and know they are effective. There are additional practices that may also be effective, but are not included because I have not experienced them. For example, I have heard wonderful things about the Chinese practice of Qi Gong, meant to develop Chi, a mysterious energy field around the body. Terri, a friend who practices martial arts with the rank of third-degree black belt, has told me that she can knock an opponent halfway across the room with a light push when she has raised her level of Chi. I believe her, but have not included a discussion of Qi Gong because I have not experienced it myself.

In this section I have presented material from a variety of cultures. My goal is to reach conclusions that apply to people in general and are not restricted to a particular culture or socioeconomic level.

For most of the techniques described here it is important to be relaxed. Mentally scan your body to locate any areas of tension, and then tell those areas to relax. Stretching a few times and then gently shaking each limb in turn is helpful. Areas of tension interfere with the relaxation necessary to get the full benefit from the practices outlined here, and as mystics point out, areas of tension also block the flow of energy through the body.

Chapter Fourteen

Shamanism: The World's Oldest Spiritual Practice

One of the goals of this book is to show that spiritual yearnings are universal and many practices are common across cultures, even cultures which did not have contact with each other. Shamanism, the oldest technique for obtaining spiritual wisdom, is common among virtually all the world's cultures at various times. There are depictions of shamans in rock art estimated to be 30,000 years old.

Some associate shamanism with the use of hallucinogenic plants, but that is an error. Scholars have shown that only a small percent of shamans worldwide used hallucinogens. In addition, in many cultures where shamans do use hallucinogenic plants, it is only on rare occasions. For example, shamans among the Buriat, a Siberian people, use hallucinogenic mushrooms, but a Buriat shaman may only take them two or three times in his life.

The major goal of shamans is to master the trance state, whereby they meet helping spirits and obtain wisdom. They have several techniques for entering into trance: going into the wilderness for solitude and sensory isolation; chanting; ritual dance; and monotonous auditory stimulation at a particular frequency, usually from a drum or rattles.

Although these techniques are described here, shamanism is best learned from an experienced teacher. The psychologist Alberto Villoldo offers training in shamanism, as does Michael Harner's

Foundation for Shamanic Studies, or FSS. There are now excellent teachers throughout the U.S. and in several other countries. A benefit of Harner's approach is that he learned shamanic techniques from many cultures and then selected those techniques common to most of the cultures studied. The result is a "core shamanism" not colored by any particular culture.

This discussion is only an overview. When someone learns a bit of shamanism and incorporates it into his or her life, interesting things begin to occur. Bob, a young patient, was hiking in the mountains with his girlfriend. The sun was getting low in the sky, and they had to get back to their car at the trailhead. He remembered a central tenet of shamanism: "Everything that is, is alive." He stopped, put his hand on a large rock, greeted it and asked it for guidance. Immediately he thought to check his bearings. Taking his map and compass from his day pack, he realized that they were going the wrong way. They were able to find the correct route, but had to hike an hour in semi-darkness to reach the car. Had he not been given the thought to check his bearings, they would have had to spend an uncomfortable night in the woods without sleeping bags or a tent.

A person does not have to give up his or her religion to practice shamanism. When Buddhism moved into Tibet, many elements of the earlier Bon Po religion were incorporated, and scholars consider Tibetan Buddhism a synthesis of Buddhism and shamanism. I have seen shamanism practices among Native Americans in the southwestern U.S. and northwestern Mexico. These peoples were converted to Catholicism by Spanish missionaries, but they see no contradiction between their Catholic faith and traditional practices. Anthropologists call the religion in that area "Sonoran Catholicism."

Wilderness and Sensory Isolation

One technique used by shamans is going into the wilderness for sensory isolation. When we cease getting normal, everyday input from our sense organs into our brains for more than a couple of hours or so, strange things begin to happen in the central nervous system. Hallucinations appear. This is a problem for the military. In the U.S. Navy, deep-sea divers who use helmeted, pressurized suits must spend hours inside their suits slowly adjusting to pressure changes before and after dives. Otherwise they will suffer from "the bends." Occasionally hallucinations are a problem during these periods.

The U.S. Air Force has had at least one conference on this topic. Air Force officers have told me of hallucinatory images, often of pretty women, during lengthy flights above cloud cover. Although he did not reveal it in his first book, in the second Charles Lindberg reported that during his lonely flight across the Atlantic he saw spirits in the cockpit. Could the spirits have been real, or were they mere illusions? The ghostly forms advised Lindberg on the flight and discussed navigation problems. The spirits vanished when he received new sensory input when he saw fishing boats as he approached the coast of Ireland.

Peter Freuchen told of a great Inuit shaman, Odark, who used a combination of sensory isolation and prolonged kinesthetic stimulation to achieve trance. He went to a lonely place in the wilderness and rubbed a stone in a circle on a rock for hours. In this way two spirit helpers, little men the size of his thumb, came to him. They gave Odark clairvoyant powers—for example, knowing where game was located—and he became more helpful to his people.

Chanting

Chanting is also a powerful technique. Andrew Weil, the psychiatrist and expert on nutritional supplements, has said, "Chanting, whatever its form, is a powerful technique to change consciousness." Peter Freuchen gave an example from the Greenland Inuit. Uvanuk, a woman who became a powerful *angakok*, or shaman, went out of her hut one evening to urinate. She was terrified as she saw a ball of fire falling out of the sky toward her. She may actually have been hit by a tiny fragment of a meteorite. After she was struck, she perceived light entering her before she fell unconscious. When she came to, she began chanting a spontaneous song or poem:

> The great sea
> Moves me
> The great sea
> Sets me adrift!
> It moves me
> Like algae on stones
> In running brook water.
> The vault of heaven
> Moves me!
> The mighty weather
> Storms through my soul.
> It tears me with it
> And I tremble with joy.

Whenever Uvanuk chanted this poem she went into trance, and in her trances she had psychic powers. For example, she became aware of the secret misdeeds of everyone in her presence. When she was not in trance, she was an ordinary person with no special abilities. Many other shamans use chants to deepen and prolong a trance they enter by drumming.

Drum and Rattle

Drumming is the technique used to induce trance in most shamanic societies, and it is used to contact the most important guardian spirit, the power animal. Katie Weatherup believes that the power animal is actually a spirit guide who takes on animal form, and that is possible. The important point is that the power animal is an ally and protector. All of us who are in reasonably good health have a power animal, a helping spirit, who protects us and supports

MYSTICAL EXPERIENCES

our vitality, whether we know it or not. Without the support of a power animal, our health and good fortune would deteriorate, eventually leading to death.

Some power animals stay with us for our entire lives, but most of the time they stay for a few years and leave. Shamans believe that our cycles of good health and good fortune, alternating with periods of less good health and bad luck, are due to the presence or absence of a power animal. I wonder if the huge increase in clinical depression in America in recent decades is because people are "dis-spirited" and have lost contact with their power animals.

There are techniques for encouraging the spirit to stay, and also for finding another when ours has left. The way to meet our power animal is to make a journey to the Lower World. We do this with an experienced teacher who beats a drum at the correct frequency, which drives the electrical activity of the brain. We lie down with something over our eyes as we do this, and we recall a cave or other natural opening in the earth, enter it and make a journey until we meet an animal. At that point it is good to ask the animal if he or she is our power animal.

On my first shamanic journey I was lying on the ground while Michael Harner did the drumming. I experienced an animal coming to me and poking its snout under me to get me up, much the same as my Labrador retriever did if I tried to stay in bed too long on a cold morning. On the next exercise Michael had us pair off with someone who had had a more successful journey. The man who worked with me saw my power animal and helped me meet it. It was the same animal I had seen in the earlier exercise, an unusual animal not found in the wild in North America. These consensual validations are frequent in shamanism.

We should cultivate our relationship with our power animals by making regular journeys to visit them. Another important way is to "dance the animal." This is usually done with two rattles that have a hard, dry sound. Good ones can often be purchased at the craft shops near Native American reservations. The rattles are usually given about two shakes per second. In this technique a person dances in a clockwise circle, moving with the gait of his or her power animal and imagining that he or she is that animal. Shamans say power animals enjoy this because it gives them a chance to experience being in physical form.

An interesting aspect of shamanism is that the techniques are more successful when we do them for someone else. When I make a journey to the Lower World, it usually takes me about fifteen minutes to find my power animal. When I made a journey for my wife, I encountered an animal within a moment or two. It happened so quickly I did not trust the experience, and so I waited a few minutes. Then I asked, "Are you Nancy's power animal?" The creature replied, "Yes! What are you waiting for, dummy?"

The Journey to the Lower World

Examples of shamans helping their community occurred frequently until recent years among the indigenous Arctic peoples in the northern part of the globe, including Siberia, Alaska, Canada and Greenland. When the catch of fish and seals became scarce and the people were in need of food, the shaman or *angakoq* made a trance journey to the bottom of the sea, where he visited Sedna, or in some tribes called Tallelayu, the queen of the sea creatures.

Sedna had a difficult life when she was in human form. She had married a man who was actually a storm bird who had shapeshifted. When Sedna fled from him and was traveling away with others, her husband created a violent storm which threatened to sink their boat. To save themselves, the other passengers threw Sedna overboard. In desperation she grabbed the gunwales of the boat, but the passengers chopped off her fingers, and she sank to the bottom of the sea. There she was transformed into a goddess and given dominion over all the creatures of the sea.

MYSTICAL EXPERIENCES

In his or her journey to the sea bottom, the shaman must get by Sedna's two fierce dogs that guard the entrance of her home. Since Sedna has no fingers, she is unable to groom herself. The shaman must comb her hair and pick any lice from it, because lice were a chronic problem among the Inuit. Then the shaman asks her to provide seals and fish for his people. Observers in the Arctic have reported that after shamans made such a ritual trance journey, there was an abundant catch of seals and fish.

Counterparts to this story of a shamanic journey can be found in almost all early epic poetry. In *Gilgamesh*, which comes from Babylonia and is considered the world's oldest surviving epic poem, the narrative's hero, Gilgamesh, makes a shamanic journey to the Lower World. There he contacts the spirit of his dead friend, Enkidu, and gets advice. The Greek story of Orpheus is about a journey to the Lower World by a shaman in an attempt to retrieve the spirit of his wife. Orpheus was directed not to turn around to look at his wife on the journey back to the world, but he turned on the way back and she was lost.

There is a similar story among the Maori. The hero, Rangi-rua, was heartbroken because his wife had died. He asked his brother Kaeo to help. The two of them made a journey to the Lower World, which the Maori call "the Land of Shadows." On their journey they had to cross a river with the aid of a sinister-looking boatman. They soon found Rangi-rua's wife, but she said that since she was a spirit and he was a man, she could not return with him. She also said that a meal was being prepared for her and she had to eat it. Rangi-rua said that since she had not yet eaten in the Lower World, she could return to the World of Light. He and his brother each grabbed one of her hands and brought her across the river. The boatman tried to stop them, but the powerful Kaeo put his foot against the prow of the boatman's canoe and gave it a kick. That sent him off in the distance. When the three reached our world, the wife directed Rangi-rua to bathe her body, and then she was able to return to it. Although the outcome is different, the similarity of this shamanic tale from the Maori and the Orpheus legend continues to startle me.

In the Greek epic *The Odyssey*, Odysseus makes a journey to the Lower World, where he meets Elpenor, one of his former companions. The poet Homer provides some details on how Odysseus made the descent to the Lower World, but I wish he had given more. In the story Elpenor pleads with Odysseus to go back to the scene where he was killed. Elpenor asks that Odysseus burn the corpse with his armor, pile a grave barrow on the shore, and plant his oar on the barrow. Odysseus agrees to do so.

This story in *The Odyssey* relates to an ancient custom among Mediterranean sailors, wearing a single gold earring on the left ear. It was believed that if a man did not have a proper burial, as Elpenor asked, his spirit would have no rest. If a sailor drowned at sea, the person who found the washed-up body could have the gold earring in exchange for doing a proper burial. The belief that the corpse must have a proper burial is widespread. Among the Arapahoe, for example, the belief persists that a person's soul or spirit wanders the earth until there is a proper burial.

The epic *Beowulf* was written in the eighth century around the time Northern Europe was converting to Christianity, so it contains both pagan and Christian influences. In one episode Beowulf makes a journey under the sea to a cave where he battles and defeats a hideous water hag, the mother of the monster Grendel. On the literal level the story is impossible, but if seen as a shamanic journey to battle a malevolent spirit, it is similar to shamanic tales throughout the world. The world's older epics illustrate that in prehistory, shamanism was the pervasive spiritual practice, or religion.

Although much of the world's ancient literature emphasizes journeys to the Lower World, the Middle World and the Upper World are also important. The Upper World is the realm of spiritual teachers, and the Middle World is our everyday world. Middle

MYSTICAL EXPERIENCES

World journeys helped ancient peoples survive. In societies where hunting was a major source of food, shamans used trance journeys to locate migrating animals.

The Quechua people of Peru maintain that all three worlds are important and we must honor the gods of all three. They believe the condor is god of the Upper World, the puma is god of the Middle World, and the serpent is god of the Lower World. Many Peruvians in the Altiplano, even many who are Christian, continue to worship these three gods.

The Question of Shape-shifting

A patient was assigned to me because he freaked out when he looked in the mirror and saw a werewolf. He was coming down off a batch of bad contraband drugs and hallucinating. This was not an example of shape-shifting, but it is reminiscent of the belief in shamanic cultures that shamans can change into the shape of an animal. Some might dismiss shape-shifting as impossible, but the body is 99.999 % empty space, and only about a thousandth of one percent matter. It should not take a great deal of energy to change the shape of such a small amount of matter. Some say even that small amount of matter is actually an energy field, and the energy can be changed from one form into another.

Tales of shape-shifting occur in the folklore of most cultures. In Norse mythology the trickster god, Loki, could appear as a horse or a salmon. Shape-shifting stories are especially numerous in Celtic literature as well as among Native American peoples and Pacific Islanders. In the pre-Christian Irish epic *Tain Bo Cuailge*, two men are mentioned, Friuch and Rucht: "They were practiced in the pagan arts and could form themselves into any shape, like Mongan Mac Fiachna."

When most Americans hear the term "Taliesin" they think of Frank Lloyd Wright's estate in Green Spring, Wisconsin. Frank Lloyd Wright was of Welsh descent, and he named his home after

Taliesin, who was the greatest of the early Welsh bards. The bard was also somewhat of a shaman and had the gift of prophesy. Some stories say he was a companion of King Arthur. The story of Taliesin's birth contains multiple shape-shiftings. There was a powerful sorceress named Ceridwen who had a servant boy, Gwion. Ceridwen was making a potion in a cauldron, and the first three drops would give great wisdom, but the remainder was poison. The potion had to be cooked for a year and a day, and needed regular stirring. Gwion was assigned that task, but one day as he was stirring, some splashed on his thumb and burned him. Almost reflexively Gwion stuck his thumb into his mouth to soothe the burn.

Ceridwen went into a rage and went for Gwion to kill him. To escape her wrath, Gwion shape-shifted into a hare, but Ceridwen became a greyhound. Then Gwion shifted into a fish, but Ceridwen became an otter. Gwion became a bird, but Ceridwen became a hawk. Finally Gwion became a seed in a farmyard, thinking Ceridwen would not notice him among the others. She did notice the seed and ate it. The seed inside her caused Ceridwen to become pregnant. She was aware of it and decided to kill the child when it was born. At birth the child was so beautiful Ceridwen could not bear to kill it outright, so she put it into a leather bag and threw it into the sea. Other versions of the tale say it was a wooden tub. The child washed up on the shore of Elffin's fishing weir, and he adopted the boy. Elffin named the child Taliesin, which in Welsh means "radiant brow."

There are a people in North America who have a tradition of shape-shifting stories, the Micmac of the Canadian Maritime provinces. They are part of a large group in eastern North America who speak languages in the Algonquian family. They had skilled healers prior to European contact, and much of this wisdom continued through colonial times. Herbal medicine as well as techniques to stop bleeding and set broken bones were known throughout the tribe. More difficult cases were treated by shamans called *puoins*. In addition to shamanic techniques, some of the *puoins* used procedures that sound remarkably similar to methods used in modern psychotherapy.

The Micmac believed that the *puoins*, or any person who developed a strong bond with his helping spirit or power animal, could shift into the shape of that animal. On a visit to the Micmac reservation at Whycocomagh on Cape Breton Island off the eastern end of Nova Scotia, I asked if there were any *puoins* or others who practiced traditional medicine. I was told that there were none "because we are Christian now." There was only one man on the reservation trying to introduce traditional practices, but he was a Lakota Sioux from the West and teaching those traditions. He had a small group of followers, yet he encountered hostility from others.

In colonial America, visitors to Cherokee areas reported seeing a dance by trained bears. Cherokees who know the traditional wisdom of their people say that the dancers were not trained bears; they were men who had shape-shifted into bear form. The Cherokee, who call themselves *Tsalagi* in their own language, performed these dances to honor the bear spirit, whom they held in high regard. An important legend was the story of the Great Bear, or *Nyah-gwaheh*, who can be seen in a constellation in the sky and who marks the changing of the seasons. The dancing bear stomps out fear and ignorance.

Shape-shifting stories are especially numerous in the Melanesian and the Polynesian islands. Charles Montgomery wrote about a woman business executive in Vanuatu, previously called the New Hebrides. She received her business education in New Zealand and was modern rather than traditional in her outlook. She reported that her uncle was a sorcerer who lived on a different island from her immediate family. She said that when she was a little girl, he would often shape-shift into an owl. Then he would fly across the water and visit at night. She said that he visited often and would set down in the breadfruit tree outside her window. He told her he had to be careful not to fly over a church on his journey. Many churches had a column of energy beaming up from the roof into the sky. If he hit that energy, he might crash.

In Polynesia there are several tales of a princess falling in love with a commoner. In earlier days social stratification was rigid on many of the islands, and it was taboo for a commoner to even touch a princess. The penalty was death. The lovers often resolved this problem by shape-shifting into sharks and swimming to a nearby island. Then they would switch back into human form to make love. Afterwards they returned to their home island as sharks.

In Samoa I heard their legend of how the coconut came to the islands. In ancient times Sina of Samoa was the most beautiful woman in all Polynesia. The king of Fiji heard of Sina's legendary beauty and wanted her for his wife. He shape-shifted into the form of an eel and swam with the currents to Samoa, where he stalked Sina. This frightened her and she fled, but the eel was relentless and followed her everywhere. He scared her every time she went to get water to drink, bathe, or cook.

In desperation she finally went to the meeting place in the center of her home village. The villagers became terrified when the gigantic eel appeared. Before the entire village he apologized to Sina for scaring her. He told her he loved her, and revealed that he was the king of Fiji. He explained that he had lost his shamanic powers. Unable to shift back into human form, he was stuck as an eel. He knew he was going to die soon. He asked Sina to cut off his head after his death, plant it in the land in front of her home, and water it daily. He said a very useful tree would grow, producing large nuts with delicious juice. He told her, "Every time you raise one of the nuts and drink the juice, Sina, you will be kissing me."

Sina did as she was asked, and carefully watered the spot where the head was buried each day. Eventually a tree sprouted, the first coconut tree in Samoa. Some Samoans say with a smile, check the bottom of a coconut. You may see the face of the eel. Samoans are fond of the legend of Sina and the eel; the story is enacted at festivals and portrayed in artwork. There is a beautiful relief carving depicting the story on a wood panel in Stevenson's Bar (no relation to RLS) at Manase on the island of Savai'i.

The legend of Sina and the eel highlights the major obstacle to shape-shifting. Shamans in indigenous cultures say that shape-shifting is not difficult. It simply involves putting our energy body inside the energy body of an animal. The difficulty for modern people is the fear that we may not be able to return to human form, and like the ancient king of Fiji, be stuck in the form of another creature for the rest of our lives.

Shape-shifting has also been reported in Christianity. In his autobiography, Saint Patrick said that he once saved his life by shape-shifting. The *Ard Righ*, or High King of Ireland, had heard that some of his people were converting to Christianity, and he wanted to learn about it. He asked Patrick to visit the palace and explain the new religion. Some members of the earlier druidic religion were fearful of losing their privileges and set up an ambush. They planned to kill Patrick to prevent his meeting the king. Patrick said that he shape-shifted into a deer and ran through the woods in animal form to avoid the ambush.

There is a holy man in the south of India, Sathya Sai Baba, now elderly, who has demonstrated remarkable healing powers, and some of this work has been documented on film. I have not seen the films, but his followers insist that he can also change into animal form.

In Nepal people believe that in addition to being able to shape-shift into animals, shamans can also shape-shift into *phurbas*, a sacred ritual tool. The *phurba* is in the shape of a dagger associated with overcoming malevolent entities, and it is used in healing. In particularly sacred rituals a shaman might shape-shift into the form of a *phurba*. I was fortunate to be able to obtain a *phurba* from Bhola, who had given it a ritual bath in the sacred Lake Manasoraver and placed on Mt. Kailash for five days to absorb healing energies.

Could the stories of shape-shifting be so universal if there were not something to them? Various writers have presented shape-shifting as a metaphor for transformation; for example, some have said that women are shape-shifters because they change shape when they become pregnant. That dilutes the issue and dodges the question of whether humans can shift into animal form. John Perkins uses the term in both senses. He witnessed a shaman shape-shift into a huge bat, and Perkins also shape-shifted into an energy ball with the aid of an Amazonian shaman. Perkins also uses the term for transforming our culture into a more ecologically sustainable form.

In the 1950s Duncan Pryde, a Scotsman who settled in Canada, lived among the Inuit in a remote Arctic area for ten years while he worked as a fur buyer. He said that at a festival he saw two shamans take turns shape-shifting into polar bears and then shifting back into human form. I have tried to shape-shift but have not been successful. Felicitas Goodman, an anthropologist who made extensive studies of trance journeys and trance postures, said that she was able to shift halfway. She took on animal form above the waist but retained human form below the waist. There are cave paintings that have survived from the Stone Age which depict such half human-half animal creatures.

Chapter Fifteen

Exploring Dreams—The Royal Road to Unconscious Wisdom

Knowing of an ancient legend regarding dreams, I visited the grave of William Butler Yeats. While there my wife, Nancy, and I climbed Ben Bulben, the mountain behind the small cemetery where the poet lies buried. When we had asked locals how long the climb would take, they told us a couple of hours. It took six. Locals often underestimate time, and we had chosen a bad route. The mountain is almost a mesa with perpendicular sides. We reached a place where we could go no further and had to go back to find another route.

After we reached the top, the view was stunning. Reflected sunlight gleamed on the sea in the distance, the peaceful silence broken only by bird calls while the scent of wildflowers perfumed the air. It was worth the climb. When we returned to the base of the mountain, it was getting dark and rain began to fall. I was glad we did not have to climb down under those conditions.

I had planned to call on the rector of the Anglican church at the cemetery and ask permission to camp overnight. If he declined, I was prepared to persuade him by offering a donation for the church. Rain began to come down hard, it had gotten quite cold, and the cemetery seemed eerie. I decided the hell with it, so instead we went to a cozy restaurant in Sligo for a splendid meal.

I had wanted to sleep on Yeats' grave because of an ancient legend in Nordic and Celtic countries. If one sleeps on the grave of a great poet, and the poet comes to them in a dream, the dreamer will become a renowned poet. There is an example in the Icelandic saga, *Thorleif Jarlskald*. A shepherd, Hallbjorn, wished to become a poet, so he slept on the grave of Thorlief for several nights. At first Hallbjorn was unsuccessful. But one night he had a dream during which the grave opened and the spirit of Thorlief arose. Thorlief recited a poem and told Hallbjorn that if he recalled the poem the next day, he would go on to become a great poet. Hallbjorn did remember it, and he became a great poet during the saga times. He lived around 1000 AD.

Some poets become irate when I tell them the story of Hallbjorn. They go into a tiresome rant along the lines of *writing poetry is hard work, you have to learn the craft, there is no easy way, and you can't get there by magic.* They do not understand the power of ritual. Hallbjorn's ritual of sleeping on the grave got him started on a path. After Hallbjorn encountered the spirit of Thorlief, he would have had great motivation to learn the techniques of the craft. His later success as a poet proved he did so.

Another example of the power of ritual comes from a healer and spiritual teacher in Los Angeles, Rahul Patel. He often tells his clients and students to go home and clean out one of their closets. That ritual is a superb metaphor for getting rid of junk before starting a spiritual path.

Modern poets also use dreams for inspiration. Paul McCartney used a dream to write one of the Beatles' most beautiful songs, "Let It Be." Brian Epstein, manager of the Beatles, kept the group organized and focused, but Epstein died in August 1967. After his death the musicians had business problems, John Lennon experienced financial strain from litigation, and the group began to lose cohesion. Paul McCartney found this time depressing, and he went through his "hour of darkness."

His mother, Mary, who had died when he was fourteen, came to him in a vivid dream, giving him strength and reassurance. This inspired the beautiful "Let It Be," which sounds like a modern hymn. Many believe that the line, "In my hour of darkness mother Mary comes to me," may refer to the mother of Jesus, but the lyric was inspired by his own mother. She came to him "speaking words of wisdom, Let it be. Let it be."

Freud realized that dreams are "the royal road to the unconscious," but he was focused on finding pathology and treating it. More recently there has been an emphasis on using dreams to get to unconscious wisdom. So many artists, poets, writers, inventors and scientists have used their dreams as a source of creative ideas that recounting their stories would require a book in itself. Two examples are given here, one from science and one from the arts.

Otto Loewi (1873-1961) won the Nobel Prize for proving that nerve impulses are conducted from one nerve cell to another across a gap called the synapse by a chemical neurotransmitter. Loewi had a dream in which the definitive experiments were revealed to him. He woke from the dream, made notes, and went back to sleep. In the morning he was devastated because he could not decipher his scribbled notes. He struggled all day to remember the details of his dream, but could not. The next night he had the same dream. This time he did not delay. He went directly to his lab and began the experiments that brought him fame and the Nobel.

Robert Penn Warren (1905-1989), an outstanding poet and novelist, was the first U.S. Poet Laureate and Consultant in Poetry to the Library of Congress when that position was created in 1984. Warren would not reveal which novel, but he said of one, "I practically dreamed the whole goddamn thing, in color, with dialogue."

The following dream by an inmate reveals how dreams can be the source of personal insights:

Shakin'

I'm in this field with big grass and lots of bushes, and I'm runnin' 'cause this thing is chasin' me. It's big and it don't have no head. It starts catchin' me and I fall, rollin' over on my back. I'm layin' there lookin' up with this thing standing over me and it's got my shotgun, the one I used to rob with. I'm lookin' down the barrel of my shotgun, then I wake up, and I'm shakin'.

With the inmate I used a technique developed by Carl Jung and later refined by Fritz Perls and the Gestalt therapists. I asked him to re-tell it, but this time switch roles. Tell the dream as if he were the monster and mention himself as Vince and not as "I" or "me." As he told the dream, taking the monster's role, he had a powerful insight. He realized that when he was doing his armed robberies he was like a monster with no head. Having no head meant he was not thinking about consequences. He realized that during his robberies he had become dangerous. Because of his dream, he knew that if he continued to rob, he would eventually have to kill or get killed.

Another example of the wisdom in dreams comes from a man, an affluent young professional rather than an inmate. He was having the same short but revolting dream repetitively, every week or two for several months. In his dream he was sitting on a toilet defecating. Then he leaned forward, reached down and grabbed a piece. He brought it up to his mouth and took a bite of it. Then the dream ended.

I said, "In your dream you are eating shit. What do men mean when they say, 'I felt like I was eating shit'?"

"Well, it means not standing up for yourself. Letting yourself get walked on."

"Is there any place where you do that in your waking life?"

"Wow! Everywhere. With my wife, on the job, with friends. If I'm going to a movie and someone cuts in front of me in the line, I don't say anything."

I began teaching the man assertiveness exercises. Since the pendulum can swing to the opposite side when we correct any problem, I worked on the difference between assertiveness and aggressiveness. We also did some role playing in the office. For example, I pretended to cut in front of him in a line and he had to speak up in an assertive way. Once he began speaking up for himself in his personal life, he stopped having the dream.

Another example of metaphor in dreams came from the sad case of a man who had been a heavy smoker for years. At the time I saw him, he was slowly dying of chronic obstructive pulmonary disease. He had this dream:

I was standing at a chasm with sparkling blue water below. There was a pretty woman in a sexy bikini on the other side, smiling and waving at me. Then she dove into the water. When she came up, she beckoned me to join her. I dove, but as I was halfway down, the water disappeared. I saw nothing but rocks and dried blood below.

This grim dream is a metaphor for the seductive but deadly results of smoking.

It is helpful to share our dreams with someone we trust. This is beneficial because we all can be a little dense in seeing the point of our own dream when it may be clear to another. Dan, a patient, had a dream that he could not understand. His wife got it and helped him understand it. Dan was in his mid fifties at the time and had dreamed he was in a gym on a table like those trainers use when working on an athlete. Dan had been a track runner in high school, and he was close to his coach, who had been a good mentor. In the dream the long-deceased coach was trimming Dan's toenails and looking down at Dan with an annoyed expression. Then the dream ended.

Dan's wife asked, do toenails mean anything to you? Dan said no, but then he suddenly remembered that his coach had emphasized having trimmed toenails prior to a race. Toenails too long may create pain that might even go unnoticed consciously, but detract from the runner's best time. Even a second or two can mean the difference in winning a close race.

Dan still did not get the point, but his wife asked, "In your dream your coach was annoyed because you hadn't trimmed your toenails. Is there anything that you should be taking care of, but you're neglecting?" Then Dan got it. There was an important project that he was avoiding.

Some claim that dreams are only the result of random firing of neurons in the brain stem and brain itself. In their view, dreams have no meaning. These people tend to be biological reductionists who do not think in metaphors, and dreams are often in metaphor. It is interesting that the three giants in dream interpretation all grew up in German-speaking areas. Sigmund Freud (1856-1939) lived in Vienna most of his life. Carl Jung (1875-1961) came from the German-speaking part of Switzerland, and Fritz Perls (1893-1970) was from Berlin. All three were required to study Goethe in the original while in high school. The subtleties of metaphors are often lost in translation. These men were well acquainted with the brilliant metaphors of one of the world's great writers.

A dramatic metaphor came from one of my adolescent patients. He was a bright and creative young man with outstanding grades in the subjects he liked, and he was a good athlete. He was also suspended from school on several occasions for fights. There had been some substance abuse, and he hung out with a group of semi-delinquents.

He had an important dream that he thought was meaningless until we worked on it. In the dream he ordered a new pair of athletic shoes, but when the shoes arrived they were mismatched. The two shoes were completely different models. I pointed out that it was a perfect metaphor for his life. On one hand he had a great intellect and had the potential to achieve wonderful goals, but on the other hand he hung out with a group of guys who were "going for bad." One path led to achievement, the other to jail. Like the shoes, his life contained two models that did not match.

MYSTICAL EXPERIENCES

Often it takes time to understand a metaphor. Although it was not a dream, one of the best examples of this came from a patient who attended a Quaker meeting. In the meeting there was a period of silent mediation, and afterwards the participants were encouraged to share any insights they received. A woman stood up and said, "If you are making a cake and put in an egg, it will be a good cake. If you put two eggs in, it will be a really good cake. But if you put in three eggs, that's just a waste." Then the woman sat. The patient thought this was a bizarre and meaningless response. Later he realized it was a wise parable about moderation.

Not all dreams are in mysterious metaphors. Dreams which are premonitions or warnings are often literal. Often predictive dreams have a *déjà vu* sense about them. The following dream came from an inmate:

Monday night I had a dream where I saw Hank get banked on the compound. (The term "banked" means a group of men gang up on and attack one man.) The next day I saw him get banked just like in the dream.

The inmate who told me about this was upset by it because he had done nothing to help the man. This man felt guilty, but his options were limited. If he had informed the guards, he would have been labeled a snitch and he would be at risk for getting banked himself. Inmates sometimes become protective of their therapists, but warn them with innuendo. An inmate told one of my colleagues, "It would be a good idea if you took tomorrow off and didn't come to work."

The next example of a warning in a dream comes from Rita Dwyer, a scientist. Early in her career she was doing research to develop an improved rocket fuel. There was an accident in the lab and she was suddenly engulfed in flames. A coworker in the next office, Ed Butler, heard her scream, and although he was not wearing any protective gear, he rushed in. He saw that her foot was the only part of her body not in flames, so he grabbed it. He pulled her under the nearby lab safety shower and yanked the cord. Water doused the flames. Rita was saved, although she had to undergo painful skin grafts. Later she asked Ed how he had known exactly what to do and do it so quickly. He told her he had had a dream a few nights earlier that mirrored the accident. After Rita recovered, she changed careers and became a therapist.

Another function of dreams is to facilitate cohesion. In many indigenous cultures families discuss dreams from the prior night over breakfast. This is a wonderful custom because, like the man in the cake story, we all can be a little dense about getting the meaning of the metaphors. In addition, areas of tension in the family can be dealt with in a non-confrontational manner. When the correct metaphor is suggested, there is a physical response. The person's posture and facial expression show that he or she has had an "a-ha" experience.

Another technique for understanding our dreams comes from the personality theorist Calvin Hall. He suggested that we write each dream on an index card and every few weeks, sort the cards by theme. Frequent themes are areas that need to be addressed. If anger or conflict comes up frequently, that area needs attention. If we are alone in most of our dreams, even though people may be passing by, we may be isolated and need to work on relating to others.

Recurrent Nightmares

Since recurrent nightmares are a serious problem for many people, that topic should be included in a discussion of dreams. This is from an inmate:

I used to get these weird dreams that scared the shit out of me, so I took drugs to stay awake and not sleep. I'd take "bam" or I'd fire cocaine, mainlining it, over ampin' so I didn't sleep for days. Once I didn't sleep for seven days and it fucked me up. I first realized something was wrong when I had trouble with my car. I had the hood open an' this guy came over to help. When he tried to

MYSTICAL EXPERIENCES

look in, I tried to stab him in the back with my screwdriver, but my brother grabbed my arm.

When we started to drive home I felt like the people in other cars were starin' at me, so I really took off. My brother said he better drive, an' I got down on the floor so they couldn't see me. He took me home an' I started watchin' TV, but I thought the guy telling the news was watchin' me. I turned the dial to make the screen black, but I could hear his voice an' it seemed like he was talkin' to me.

I went up to the bedroom an' locked myself in. My wife called my mother and father, and they took me to the hospital. When they got me home I locked myself in the bedroom again for a few days, but it was weeks before I was all right. Cocaine, bam, an' not sleepin' can really make you get paranoid.

People with recurrent nightmares often respond like this inmate and try to avoid sleep. A wise writer on spirituality, Barbara Brown Taylor, gave an example of a middle-class man who had a recurring nightmare that kept him from having a good night's sleep for years. Although he did not have the dream every night, he had it often enough that he was on guard against it every night. In his dream a demon showed up at his door and banged so hard the door bulged. The man grabbed something to kill the demon, but every time he killed it the demon got bigger. During the struggle a piece of the demon would fall onto him, and he would become part of the demon. He would wake up so soaked in sweat that the bed linens were wet.

During the dream one night the man got the idea that the demon wanted a blessing from him. In the dream the man gave him a blessing, but the demon was eager for more, and the man did it many times. Finally the man added, "Now go in peace." The demon made a sound like a kitten and never showed up again.

Both of these cases illustrate an important message. Trying to avoid sleep is an ineffective strategy for dealing with nightmares.

The nightmare must be confronted, but not as our enemy. In a way the nightmare is our friend, trying to tell us something we need to know about ourselves that we had been avoiding. The man who blessed the demon in Barbara Brown Taylor's story was accepting the demon as part of himself in a symbolic way. Once we accept our demons, they no longer have power over us.

Post Traumatic Stress Disorder, or PTSD, nightmares are a type of recurring nightmare that requires the help of a mental health professional. They are repetitions of the traumatic event rather than metaphors. When the nightmares have not occurred for some time and then suddenly recur, the precipitating event is often a metaphor for the original trauma. A combat veteran went several years without nightmares, but they recurred during a hospital stay. They were so severe that his bed linens were so soaked in sweat they had to be changed before he could go back to sleep.

In his traumatic event he and four other soldiers were pinned down by machine gun fire. They took refuge in a shallow crater from artillery fire, but they were stuck, and anyone who tried to go forward or back was killed. During this patient's hospital stay he was diagnosed with a fatal condition that progressed slowly. Once again, he was stuck and could neither go forward or backward. That precipitated nightmares of the old trauma.

Most of the time our dreams and nightmares bring messages from the unconscious mind that need to come into conscious awareness. In parts of Asia there is a saying: "An unexamined dream is like an unopened letter." Although the message is usually in metaphor, which needs interpretation, our dreams bring wisdom from our unconscious into consciousness. Our dreams tell us things we need to hear.

Chapter Sixteen

Meditation—The Queen of the Mind Development Techniques

A male patient who had begun morning meditation a few months earlier said one day when the alarm went off, he did not want to get up. He was tired and the room was chilly. He decided he'd skip meditation that day and stay in the warm bed a bit longer. Then he heard a pleasant female voice say, "Aren't you going to come visit?" He does not know if the voice was an expression of his own unconscious or it came from a spiritual source.

Sharon Janis, a remarkably clear and concise writer on spirituality, has said that meditation is turning down the outside noise and inner chattering so we can hear the voice of God. Those who do not believe in God may think it is your own inner wisdom that you hear, but at one level the source does not matter. Meditation leads to wisdom, and that is why the Buddha made it one of the eight steps on the path he laid out for his followers.

There are also remarkable physical benefits from meditation. It helps you relax, and it relieves anxiety along with the effects of stress. There have been enough long-term longitudinal studies of meditation to show that on average, a group that practices meditation on a daily basis lives several years longer than control groups who are matched on age, gender, physical activity, etc.

A powerful description of meditation comes from Peter Freuchen, the Danish physician and explorer who lived among the Greenland Inuit for eleven years:

On the rock of Agpat, behind Thule, where the dead ones were stone set, I often saw men and women in quiet meditation. On these occasions they would dress in their newest and most beautiful clothes, and then sit quite still, staring out over land and sea for hours on end. They believed that during this stillness they received the wisdom of their ancestors.

Unfortunately, in our culture there is a tendency to treat stress, anxiety and tension with a pill rather than by teaching a patient to meditate. A man in his early thirties contacted me for psychotherapy for an anxiety problem. Two and a half years earlier he had seen his physician, who prescribed Xanax, a tranquilizer in the benzodiazepine family. He became dependent, and when the patient tried to go off the medication he was unsuccessful. In his words, "It was hell," and he resumed taking it.

I am not opposed to medication, and I am quick to refer a patient when medication is needed, but that particular drug should be used only short term when the problem is acute. I coordinated with his physician and taught the patient meditation and other anxiety reduction techniques while he slowly titrated down on his dosage. It took him a full year to overcome his dependence and go off the drug completely.

Meditation is practiced within most religions, including Buddhism, Hinduism, Christianity, Judaism, Islam, Sikhism, Taoism, and the Bahai'i faith, as well as within secular groups. There is even a Wiccan form of meditation. Needless to say, this has resulted in a wide variety of techniques. In the U.S. there have been a number of fads in meditation. During the 1950s and early '60s, Zen became popular among literary types and those attracted to the "beat" or "beatnik" scene. This was due to the influence of writers such as Alan Watts and the poets Allen Ginsberg and Gary Snyder.

Later in the 1960s Transcendental Meditation, or TM, which used mantras or Sanskrit words, was developed by an ascetic in India, Maharishi Mahesh Yogi. The popularity of this method

MYSTICAL EXPERIENCES

soared after the Beatles and the Beach Boys went to India to learn the technique. Those musicians felt TM enhanced their creativity and enabled them to better resist drugs and alcohol, perennial temptations in the pop music scene. Hundreds of thousands of Americans learned TM at the peak of its popularity in the 1970s, and TM continues to have practitioners, but in smaller numbers. Although not as popular as TM at its peak, in recent years Vipassana, the "mindfulness" method, has attracted many of my colleagues within the mental health professions.

Which of these techniques work, and which is best? They all work, and the best one is the one you stick with and practice every day. Meditation is like an exercise program. At first it takes discipline to do it every morning, but with time you grow to enjoy it. When a problem prevents you from doing it on a particular day, you feel that you missed something important, and you want to get back to it.

I am not an expert on meditation, and these comments are only an introductory outline. Meditation should be learned from a teacher, because disturbing images can come up. Jack Kornfield, a psychologist and meditation teacher, told the story of an overzealous young man who attended a meditation retreat. He went off on his own and meditated continuously for a day and a half. When he returned to the meditation hall, he had a panic attack. He believed that he could see the past lives of everyone present, and this overwhelmed him. If you believe there are no teachers in your area, do not worry. In India there is a proverb: "When the student is ready, the teacher appears."

A caveat should be mentioned. Meditation is a great technique for mental development, but it is not a panacea, because there are no panaceas. I know people who have practiced meditation for decades but continue to carry excessive emotional baggage. One man, who is a well-qualified teacher of meditation, believes that psychotherapy is unnecessary if one meditates enough. He is over fifty but still carries a huge amount of resentment against his parents. All parents make mistakes, and some are abusive, either because they themselves were abused as children or they carry pathology. These issues need work and some painful introspection. Eventually we must let go of the resentment and forgive our parents. It is one of the life tasks we all need to complete to finish growing up, reach full adult maturity, and get on with our own lives. That meditation teacher carries a burden he needs to drop.

Zen Meditation

Recently I saw a concrete example of the benefits of meditation. I stayed at a bed and breakfast guest house run by a group of Zen practitioners in Boulder, Colorado. The staff all practiced meditation, as did a few of the guests, but most of the guests did not. The difference between those who meditated versus those who did not was clear; it was as if the two groups wore the different-colored jerseys of two opposing teams. Whether they were staff or guests, those who meditated appeared present, centered and composed. Those guests who were not into meditation were often preoccupied or talked with pressure of speech, which indicates tension.

One guest who did not meditate had severe pressure of speech and told an endless stream of lame jokes, another sign of excess tension. He also blamed an anonymous "they" for his misfortunes, including the fire he started which burned down his house. "They" did not tell him it was dangerous to build too big a fire in his fireplace and overheat an uncleaned chimney. Blaming others and failing to take responsibility for one's behavior is a sign of immaturity. I checked my guesses by asking people if they practiced meditation, and my hunch was correct every time. Meditation and psychotherapy work on different levels within a person, and they complement each other.

MYSTICAL EXPERIENCES

Counting the Breaths

There are different techniques within Zen, but all involve correct posture, breathing, and relaxation. The most common method, and perhaps the easiest to learn, involves counting the breaths. The student sits cross-legged on a cushion, which is placed on a rectangular mat. Those who are not flexible enough use a small bench. Attention is focused on the sensation of air passing into and out of the nose.

Most people close the eyes halfway, breathe slowly and deeply, and count the breaths on the exhale. Japanese count them to ten and start over. Westerners tend to count the breaths to four and then start over, although some have learned to count to ten in Japanese and do it that way. If attention wanders, or if the person starts to doze, attention should be brought back to the breath. An alternate way is to simply sit in the meditation posture on the cushion, relaxed but alert, for the specified length of time, usually twenty or thirty minutes.

Rinzai and Koans

The Rinzai branch of Zen is considered the most rigorous. One friend has referred to it as the Marine Corps of Zen Buddhism. In addition to practicing standard Zen meditation, students are given a "koan," or puzzle that must be solved with the intuitive rather than the logical mind. Houston Smith said, "Koans are Zen riddles that you do not solve so much as step through, as through Alice's looking glass into Mad Hatterish conundrums designed to stun rational sense and in its place induce wordless insight."

The following is an example of a koan: A master teacher in China, Joshu, was giving a talk on Buddha nature, and a student asked if dogs have Buddha nature. The master answered, "Mu," which is a not a word in Chinese. Based on this story, what is the meaning of "Mu"? Another koan is "What is the sound of one hand clapping?"

Students are given their koans by Zen masters, and the students often work on them for months or even years. There are many stories of a student struggling with a koan for years, and getting a flash of insight when something unexpected happens. One man who had been unsuccessful for a year and a half was waiting to see the master on a frosty winter morning. The student slipped on a patch of ice, and when he hit the ground, he had a sudden flash of insight, a small *satori*, and he knew the solution to his koan.

I admit to once misusing a koan. I had been asked to see an inmate with a severe anxiety problem. He had the worst pressure of speech I have seen. In our first session it became apparent that he was using his logorrhea as a defense so he would not have to look at more painful issues. As a way of getting him to slow down on the speech and reflect, at the end of the session I told him that at our next meeting I wanted him to tell me, "What is the sound of one hand clapping?" Two days later I had to see another man in that part of the jail. When I walked past the inmate's cell, he was staring at his right hand, opening it and snapping it shut. Of course that is not the answer, but I hope he persists in working on the koan and it leads to some spiritual awakening.

These few comments hardly do justice to the vast amount of wisdom within Zen. I enjoy their repertoire of marvelous teaching stories. A story about doing things one-pointedly involves a man who tried to save time in the morning by holding his penis with one hand and urinating in the toilet while he brushed his teeth with the other hand. He did not do a good job on his teeth, and when he missed the toilet he created a mess he had to clean up.

Mantra Meditation

I believe mantra meditation is the easiest form to learn, so it is the one I practice. Since I am not flexible enough to sit in the full or half lotus position, I sit on a low stool without a back. If I start to doze, I start to fall and that wakes me.

MYSTICAL EXPERIENCES

Mantras are words or phrases, usually in Sanskrit, repeated silently or sometimes chanted. The Sanskrit phrases are said to have vibrational power affecting the mind and body. This may be true. Everything in the world has a resonance frequency, and a sound at the same frequency as an object's resonance frequency, or a harmonic of that frequency, will cause that object to vibrate. Many have seen the video of the opera singer sustaining a note while a nearby wine glass vibrates and then shatters. Since the time of the Napoleonic wars, marching troops break out of step when crossing a bridge because the vibration matched the resonance frequency of a particular bridge and caused it to collapse some 200 years ago.

Mantras do not have to be in Sanskrit. The nineteenth century poet laureate of England, Alfred, Lord Tennyson, would chant his own last name over and over until he entered that magical state for writers when the words flow and the sense of time disappears.

A mantra can be obtained from a teacher, or by perusing one of the books on mantras until you are attracted to a particular one and it grabs you. Another way is to take a Transcendental Meditation, or TM, course. TM is pricey—at one point the fee reached $2500—but I am told it has been reduced to become more competitive with other methods. For the initial meeting the student is asked to bring flowers, soft fruit, and a clean handkerchief as an offering. The student is assigned a short mantra according to a formula based on the student's age and gender. Then the student is taught to say the mantra quietly while breathing slow and deep.

If attention wanders, the student is taught to bring attention back to the mantra, but not to fight intruding thoughts because that gives them power. Instead the student is taught to just let the thoughts go by, like sitting on a hillside watching cars go by in a valley below, not becoming attached to thoughts of any particular car. The eventual goal is to achieve "consciousness without object."

A graduate student who moved to a home near the busy New York-to-Florida train route said that at first the noise from the trains was quite annoying, but eventually he stopped noticing it. Similarly, after some time the meditation student has brief periods when he or she ceases to notice the mantra and reaches moments of pure awareness, a blissful state.

TM, created by Maharishi Mahesh Yogi (1917-2008), has had great popular success, with close to a million practitioners in the U.S. alone. Popular musicians, including the Beatles, especially Paul McCartney and Ringo Starr, and the Beach Boys are among those who practiced TM. Movie directors such as Clint Eastwood and David Lynch are also followers. It is rumored that some members of the U.S. Congress practice TM. For a time the Maharishi had celebrity status.

Unfortunately, fame is a bitch goddess. The public loves the person who ascends, but after an interval on the peak, the crowd becomes bored and wants to de-throne the star. Unfounded allegations can be made, or harmful personal information, such as financial or sexual indiscretions, can be revealed. The main charges against the Maharishi were that he was leading a cult, and that he was doing a stealth job of sneaking the Hindu religion into America, getting people to worship Hindu gods and goddesses.

These allegations are unfair. It is true that some of the mantras given in TM are the names of Hindu deities; for example, the mantra Shyam is one of the names of Krishna. It is not Krishna who is being worshipped when a person repeats or chants "Shyam." The meaning of the word is unimportant; the vibrational power of the sound is central. In addition, most Westerners are not aware that the Hindu religion is monotheistic beneath a polytheistic cover. The various gods and goddesses are different manifestations of the One Intelligence, so supreme and complex that it cannot be grasped by the human mind. As Houston Smith has shown, Hinduism and the Judeo-Christian religions are remarkably similar at their core.

Spiritual movements reflect the cultural context of the area where they emerged. TM emerged from the spiritual traditions of

MYSTICAL EXPERIENCES

India, and it reflects those traditions. The only spiritual practice that is relatively culture free is Michael Harner's teachings on shamanism. The Maharishi deserves credit for teaching a form of meditation that is easily learned and accessible to the general public. Charles Tart, a respected research psychologist, tried to learn other forms of meditation, but was unsuccessful. He was able to learn TM and found it gave him increased ability to concentrate, spontaneous processing of unfinished business, increased tolerance of cold, and decreased tolerance of alcohol.

Other Forms of Mantra Meditation

Deepak Chopra, the physician and spiritual teacher, practiced TM for years, but recently began marketing his own competing technique, called "Primordial Sound Meditation." In Chopra's technique, the vibrational quality of the sound enables the student to slip into the gap between thoughts, beyond the constant internal chatter and into pure awareness. This is similar to TM's "consciousness without object." It costs approximately $375, still pricey but more affordable than TM.

Another interesting technique was developed by the Boston cardiologist Herbert Benson. Benson's early research helped to document many of the health benefits of TM, but because of concern about Hindu mantras in TM, he developed an alternative technique. In Benson's approach, which he calls "The Relaxation Response," the word "one" is used as a mantra. Those with a secular orientation who feel uncomfortable with the Hindu terms in TM often like Benson's approach.

Candle Meditation

Lighting a candle is an important act in most of the world's religions, and light from the candle is seen as a metaphor for the presence of God. I was impressed by an incident at a modern workshop on shamanism sponsored by the Foundation for Shamanic Studies.

A Navajo woman hesitantly came into the hall at the beginning of the workshop, and she looked skeptical. When she saw the lit candle on the small altar in the center of the room she said, "Oh, I'm glad to see some fire." Then she relaxed. As the workshop progressed, she became an enthusiastic participant.

Teachers in India compare the untrained human mind to a drunken monkey, constantly jumping from one thought to another without the ability to stay focused and concentrate. Although the focal point is visual rather than sound, candle meditation is like a mantra. It uses an object to focus the mind, and eventually the object fades out and we have periods of pure awareness. Candle meditation is an ancient technique. Patanjali mentioned it approximately 2000 years ago, but at that time it had already been practiced for centuries.

In simple candle meditation, one puts a candle in a safe holder on a low table about five feet away. Those flexible enough may sit in a cross-legged position, but I prefer to use a low stool without a back. If I begin to doze off, I start to fall and that awakens me. Direct your attention to the flame. If intruding thoughts drift in, let them be there and gently bring attention back to the flame. We may see other things in the flame. One friend sees a little man.

An advantage of candle meditation is that we can continue to see the flame if we close our eyes because of the retinal afterimage. Because it is so relaxing, some people do it for a few minutes as a prelude to regular meditation. Others like to take a short nap afterwards, making sure to first extinguish the flame.

Vipassana, or Mindfulness Meditation

Vipassana meditation, sometimes called insight meditation or mindfulness, comes from the southern form of Buddhism found mainly in Sri Lanka, Thailand, and Myanmar (Burma). Just as one need not be a Hindu to practice mantra meditation, one need not be a Buddhist to practice Vipassana, although it is based on the teachings of Buddha as preserved in the *Pali Canon,* the oldest extant written text of Buddha's teachings. Vipassana is popular among mental health professionals. One editor of a psychology journal became so partial to publishing articles on Vipassana that readers who wanted a wider scope of articles began suggesting he change the name of the publication to *The Journal of Indic Studies.*

Vipassana meditation is more complex than mantra meditation and is best learned from a course or a private teacher. There are one-day introductory workshops, ten-session courses, and a ninety-session online course. A comparison to mantra meditation is not reasonable, because Vipassana is a way of life rather than limited to the practice of meditation. Some call Vipassana meditation "The Art of Living."

There are moral precepts in Vipassana, which include refraining from killing other creatures; refraining from stealing; refraining from sexual misconduct (sexual action that hurts another); refraining from lying and harmful speech; and restraint with alcohol and recreational drugs. The Buddha believed that wisdom cannot be fully developed without a foundation of moral behavior.

There are two components of Vipassana meditation: concentration, or the ability to focus attention one-pointedly, and developing insight and wisdom by seeing the true nature of reality. The practice begins with sitting cross-legged on the floor or a cushion and observing the rise and fall of the abdomen with the inhale and exhale of the breath. This should be observed without trying to control the breath. Intruding thoughts are not to be labeled; for example, if one notices the bark of a dog, it should be considered "sound."

If an itch occurs, one should note the itch and the desire to be free of it. The intention of moving the hand is noted, as well as the movement to the itchy spot, along with the scratching. The movement of the hand back and the placement of the hand back in the lap is also noted. The new feeling when the itch has gone is also noted, and then attention returns to the rising and falling of the abdomen. A similar procedure is used for thoughts, emotions, or mental images that come up.

When I took a workshop on Vipassana, I developed a feeling similar to the one I get when hypnotized. I have taken several hypnosis classes over the years in which the students paired off and practiced techniques on each other. One technique that works well on me is based on the limits of the human mind to process information. It is hard to keep more than seven to nine things in mind at the same time. Some psychologists call this "the magic number seven, plus or minus two."

The next time you host a large dinner party, note that if the number of guests exceeds five to seven, conversation will break into two separate groups. For myself and many others, if I try to be aware of too many things at the same time, my mind says, "Enough, enough," and I go into a light trance. I have discussed this with people who know a great deal more than I about Vipassana, and most, but not all, have agreed with me.

Daily Activities as Meditations: Eating and Walking

There are two other forms of meditation which developed within the Vipassana tradition: walking meditation, which is used throughout Southeast Asia; and eating meditation.

If more than one person is practicing walking meditation, it is good to divide the area into lanes. A few stretches and shaking of the limbs to relax before starting is also helpful. Before beginning, the posture should be noted, as well as the intention to walk. One should be mindful or aware of the process. The right foot should be lifted in a fluid movement from beginning to end. The placement of the right foot back on the ground is to be noted as "placing." Then the left foot is lifted and moved in a smooth arc. There is a pause of about a second between steps, and only one foot is moved at a time. At the end of the path "stopping" is noted, and then the intention to turn. Then there is a pivot on the right heel while noting the turning. Then the whole process is repeated.

Needless to say, walking meditation takes more time than usual walking, but those who practice it treasure it. Walking becomes more calm and graceful, and this spreads to other areas of life. Buddhist teachers say walking meditation can be as effective as sitting meditation, and it helps the person learn to stay in the present moment.

Most of us eat too fast without paying attention to the sensations involved, and we tend to take the next bite too soon, before we have completely finished chewing and swallowing the first bite. Even those who do not have an eating disorder have tensions about food. Eating meditation is valuable correction, and some therapists teach it to patients as a weight loss technique. Many say that it also reduces their need for antacids or acid blockers.

In eating meditation the student is mindful or aware of the steps and sensations in eating. As one goes to the table, there is awareness of intention to eat, approaching the table, grasping the chair, pulling it out, and sitting. The posture should be noted, any sensations of hunger and desire for food. Gripping the fork or utensil, picking up food with the fork, moving it to the mouth, noting the tastes and sensations, including the aromas, mouth feel and texture, are all part of the process. Chewing should be thorough, and the fork put down on the plate until chewing is finished and the food swallowed before the next piece is taken.

Needless to say, meals take longer when eaten mindfully. At meditation retreats they can take two hours, but in everyday life an hour or slightly less is a reasonable goal. At times you become impatient and want to eat faster; one should note this desire but not give in to it. When the meal is finished, one should remain for a bit and note the sensations in the body. While paying attention to all the details during the meal, some people cease to be aware of what they are eating. I was surprised to learn that the Buddhist teachers consider this a positive step.

Meditation and Techniques to Cultivate Creativity

There are a number of techniques that enhance creativity, and all of them involve quieting the mind. Dreams have already been discussed, and obviously the mind is quieted during sleep. The technique that has been the object of the most scientific study over the past several decades is meditation. Several scientists have concluded that creativity is enhanced by meditation. Nancy C. Andreasen, a prominent research psychiatrist who has done outstanding work on creativity, has said that in addition to the other benefits of meditation, it is a "useful resource for thinking more creatively." Many followers of the various schools of meditation would agree. Andreasen stated that meditation has beneficial effects on brain function that can be measured with scientific instruments.

Recent studies on creativity have focused on gamma waves, which are high-frequency oscillations produced in the brain. When these waves occur in different brain regions at the same time, the brain is integrating complex information to solve a problem or find a core pattern. Andreasen said that when a group of Buddhist monks were studied, they had high levels of gamma synchronicity, and the amount of gamma synchronicity was correlated with the amount of time the particular monk had spent practicing meditation. The gamma waves in the monks were strongest in the associative cortex of the brain, especially in the frontal and side areas of the brain. Andreasen believes that these areas of the cortex are the reservoir of creativity.

Creativity is a two-stage process. The first is getting the creative idea, and the second is producing a finished result, which requires mastery of technique and hard work. Thomas Edison called these stages the "inspiration" and the "perspiration." Learning craftsmanship and technique are straightforward, but getting the

MYSTICAL EXPERIENCES

inspiration is more elusive. Having spent time on Pacific islands, I enjoy the paintings of Paul Gauguin, but they are unaffordable. I paid a competent artist to copy one, and it is a good reproduction, but it lacks the creative spark. When I see Gauguin's paintings in museums, they feel alive.

To get that spark of inspiration, creative people throughout the ages have known it was important to quiet the mind and listen to the inner voice. In his painting in the Sistine chapel, Michelangelo includes both the major and the minor prophets of the Bible. Angels are at the ears of all of them, but only the major prophets are listening. Composers have also realized the importance of quieting the surface mind to experience creativity. Puccini (1858-1924), who wrote the masterpieces *La Boheme* and *Madame Butterfly*, told his biographer:

> He (the composer) must acquire... technical mastery of his craft, but he will never write anything of lasting value unless he has Divine aid also. There is a vast amount of good music paper wasted by composers who don't know this simple truth.

Johannes Brahms (1833-1897), a great composer of the Romantic Period, made a similar comment. He said that much of his music came to him from God, but he had to be in a "semi-trance" condition to get results. He also said that the conscious mind had to be in temporary abeyance, and it was "through the subconscious mind, which is part of the omnipotence, that inspiration comes."

It is interesting that both Puccini and Brahms considered these points sacred and intensely personal. In separate incidents both Puccini and Brahms revealed this material to their biographers only on the condition of a fifty-year delay before these comments were published. Did Puccini and Brahms get Divine aid, or once they quieted their minds, did they access creativity from their own unconscious? The answer to that question is beyond my ken.

There are numerous reports, both ancient and modern, of various inventors and artists using meditative techniques to foster their creativity. Thomas Edison's niece said that he meditated before beginning work in the lab. Many of the great poets used meditation to quiet the mind and access creativity. Basho (1644-1695), who many Japanese consider their greatest poet, meditated, as did Takahashi (1901-1987). William Butler Yeats (1865-1939) expressed gratitude to the British group that taught him meditation. The contemporary American poets Gary Snyder and Jane Hirshfield practice Zen meditation.

In earlier times poets did not receive their incomes from college teaching or book sales. They had patrons, nobles who supported them by commissioning works, and the poets had to create on demand. There had to be a poem praising the patron's bravery after a battle, laments had to be composed when a family member died, and love poems needed to be written for engagements and marriages. Although it was not called meditation, an English visitor in 1695 gave the following report on the practices of Scottish poets:

> I must not omit to relate their way of Study, which is very singular: They shut their Doors and Windows for a day's time, and lie on their backs, with a stone upon their belly, and Plads about their Heads, and their Eyes being cover'd, they pump their Brains for Rhetorical Encomium or Panegyrick; and indeed they furnish such a stile from this dark cell, as is understood by very few.

It is doubtful that the poems were not understood by the patron, or the poet would have been out of a job. It is more likely that the poet used local idioms not familiar to the visitor. The practice appears to be meditation, but the stone on the belly is a puzzle. It was likely used to stop hunger pangs.

The prelude to the pre-Christian Irish epic *Tain Bo Cuailnge* illustrates the creative process. The Irish word *Tain* is usually translated as "cattle raid," but that does not do justice to the epic. It is a tale about the over-ambitious and fierce Queen Maeve. She led her army from Connacht in the west of Ireland to Cuailnge on the northeast coast to steal a prize bull with magical powers. Like many epics, the smaller stories within tell a great deal about the human condition.

In pagan times Senchan Torpeist, the chief poet of Ireland, gathered the poets to see if any recalled the entire *Tain*. Each had only parts, and none had the complete version. Senchan sent a group of poets, including his son Muirgen, to another part of the country where there was believed to be a copy. On the way the group came upon the gravestone of Fergus MacRoich, one of the more admirable figures in the epic.

While the others went to find a place to stay for the night, Muirgen sat down and chanted a poem to the stone as if it were Fergus himself. Suddenly a great mist formed around Muirgen, and for three days he could not be found. Fergus appeared in the mist, dressed royally in a green cloak and a tunic embroidered in red. Fergus wore bronze sandals and had a gold-hilted sword at his side. During the three days he recited the entire Tain. Muirgen was able to recall it and return to Senchan with the complete epic.

In a dense mist, boundaries disappear. While skiing I once entered a whiteout. It was disorienting because I could not see the horizon separating earth from sky. It would have been dangerous to continue, and I had to stop. In epics dense mists or whiteouts mean that the boundary between the world of the living and the world of the dead is also blurred. Did Muirgen encounter the spirit of Fergus? Did the story come from Muirgen's unconscious? Chanting the poem at the gravestone may have put him in a trance where he could access unconscious material. Perhaps the story came from a combination of spiritual help and Muirgen's own unconscious.

All of these stories on creativity make the same point. Muirgen, the Scottish poets, Brahms, Puccini and Michelangelo's painting all indicate that creativity is a two-step process. Mastering the techniques of the craft is essential. That is hard work which cannot be avoided. Later, we must use meditation or some other procedure to quiet the chatter of the conscious mind, get it out of the way, so we can listen to the inner voice.

Chapter Seventeen

Autogenic Training—A German Technique

In 1956 a German physician, Dr. Hannes Lindemann, startled the world with an astounding achievement that caused his photo to grace the cover of *Life* magazine, a popular weekly in the U.S. at the time. He had loaded a two-person Klepper kayak with 154 pounds of supplies and traveled across the Atlantic from the Canary Islands to a beach on St. Martin's in the Caribbean almost 3,000 miles away. He used a small sail to assist at times, but he paddled much of the way. The journey took him 72 days.

It is an understatement to say long-distance sea kayaking is hazardous. Two people recently attempted to go from Australia to New Zealand, a distance of about 1,000 miles, but they perished not far from their goal. Some remarkable features of Lindemann's voyage were that when he arrived he was in good physical shape, and after only a few moments getting used to standing on solid ground, he was able to move about unassisted.

In contrast, Ed Gillette, an expert kayaker, traveled from Monterey, California to Hawaii, a distance of 2,200 miles, in 64 days. Ed had problems with salt water sores and boils. Prolonged contact with salt water abrades the skin, allowing surface bacteria to get into more vulnerable tissue underneath. He had prepared for this by bringing a supply of hydrocortisone cream, but it was swept overboard during a patch of rough weather. When Ed arrived in Maui and stepped onto the beach, his legs crumpled under him. He had trouble standing upright and walking.

Lindemann practiced "autogenic training" for three months prior to his trip and regularly during his voyage. This is a mind-body technique originally developed in Germany by a psychiatrist, Johannes H. Schultz, who first published his work in 1932. Others, such as Wolfgang Luthe, have also made contributions. The training contains both a meditative component and a physical component that is similar to biofeedback, but without the equipment. Mystical experiences also occur. Some feel that they go out of their bodies. Others report improved relationships with their significant others even when they had not communicated with the others.

Autogenic training produces powerful physiological and psychological results, and it is particularly effective in treating illnesses caused by stress. Although the technique has not gained a large following in the U.S., it is used by some psychologists and others in the health care community. I have heard of people who were badly injured in car wrecks who used autogenic training to prevent going into shock before help arrived. They believe it saved their lives.

Standard Exercises in Autogenic Training

A reclining chair with a high back to support the head should be used. Any tight or constrictive clothing such as a belt, shoes or necktie should be loosened. If the room is cool, a light blanket should go over the patient. The patient should be told to let himself (or herself) relax and allow his limbs and body to feel warm. Any specific area of the body where there is a problem, such as a sore muscle or cramp, should be visualized and allowed to feel warm. The patient should be told that he is at peace, and to allow his body to feel heavy. In the early sessions it is recommended to start at the head and gradually proceed down the body, instructing the patient to allow each area to feel warm and heavy.

After the patient or trainee has become more relaxed, he should be instructed to tell himself, "I am at peace. My arms and legs feel heavy and warm." (Repeat this several times.) "My heart-

MYSTICAL EXPERIENCES

beat is calm and regular." (Repeat several times.) This step involves calm breathing. The trainee should say, "My breathing is calm," and eventually move on to, "It breathes me." In other words, he is not controlling his breath; it is naturally flowing through him.

Instruct the trainee to let his solar plexus (the area between the bottom of the breastbone and the navel) feel warm. The earlier steps should be repeated as part of the sequence each time a new step is added, e.g., "I am at peace. My arms and legs are heavy and warm. My heartbeat is calm and regular. It breathes me. My solar plexus is warm." Each individual phrase should be repeated at least three times.

Instruct the trainee or patient to feel that his forehead is cool and silently repeat, "My forehead is cool." It may help to instruct him to feel a cool breeze blowing across his forehead or imagine he is in a hot tub in a peaceful place. Repeat the entire sequence, adding, "My forehead is cool."

In traditional autogenic training it takes about four months to complete these six steps, and daily practice is recommended. After Step Six, the trainee is taught to go into the relaxed state quickly and to retain it despite interruptions, such as the light in the room being turned off and on, the telephone ringing, or a radio playing. This part of the program provides good protection against stress or interruptions.

The next part of the program, the Meditative Exercises, often takes another four months, or about eight months total. Although this may seem long, it should be remembered that when this method was published in 1932, the other available major treatment was psychoanalysis, which took several years. In addition, after the first few sessions of each step, the patient can do the exercises on his own.

The Meditative Exercises

1. Spontaneous Colors—In the Meditative Exercises the sessions are longer, 30 to 60 minutes. After the patient is relaxed and his eyes closed, he tends to see colors in his visual field despite his closed eyes. Blue is the most common color, and this is encouraged.

2. Selected Colors—The trainee is first told to see variations of the individual color seen in Step One; then he is told to visualize other colors. If he has difficulty, the therapist may suggest specific images, such as imagining an orange to see orange, trees to see green, or a rose to see red.

3. Visualizing Concrete Objects—After doing the relaxing steps, the trainee or patient is told to hold onto any visual images or objects that appear in his mind's eye while his eyes are closed. This exercise improves the ability to concentrate.

4. Visualizing Images Which Signify Abstract Concepts—In this stage the patient may see a bird over a hillside and think of "freedom." Other images may be dreamlike or emotionally charged. Those images are explored later in the session with psychotherapy.

5. Experiencing Particular Emotions or States of Feeling—Feelings from the past, or wish fulfillment, accompanied by visual images, occur. For example, a woman wanting to have a baby may see herself feeding a baby. Nostalgic images from the past, religious figures or archetypal images may also occur.

6. Visualizing Specific People—At this step the patient is told to visualize specific people, beginning with neutral figures who do not evoke strong emotions. Later he is told to visualize emotionally significant people. In this stage negative or hostile feelings tend to become more realistic and objective.

For most people the six standard and the six meditative sessions complete the program, but additional exercises are available for particular disorders, such as hypertension, bronchial asthma, migraine, and other conditions. Since the development of biofeed-

MYSTICAL EXPERIENCES

back therapy, these exercises are less widely used than in the past. During the advanced steps of autogenic training, people sometimes have out-of-body experiences and perceive themselves as floating above their bodies. There is no question that autogenic training works, but it has not caught on in the U.S. as it has in Germany. Americans tend to become impatient with the pace of the training. Could it be that Germans are more methodical and have the self-discipline to do the required daily practices, but Americans do not?

Chapter Eighteen

The Heart Exercise—A Taoist Technique for Healing Relationships

This Taoist heart exercise strengthens our relationships with those we love and helps to repair troubled or negative relationships. The strange and mystical aspect of this technique is that it works without any conscious awareness by the recipient. Many people have said it improved their marriages. The level of tension went down, and people who were tentative about staying in their marriages have said the heart exercise increased their commitment. Of course, the Taoist heart exercise does not replace marital counseling. The two approaches work on different levels, and the combination is more powerful than either one alone.

Various spiritual teachers present slightly different versions of the heart exercise, but I prefer that of Stephen Russell, the English spiritual teacher and martial arts expert. He sometimes writes under the name "The Barefoot Doctor." This name refers to the paramedics in China, not literally barefoot, who provide health care in rural areas without physicians.

Russell recommends first doing this exercise on someone we love, to obtain practice and become familiar with it. We visualize an opening, an orifice in the center of our chest in the heart area. We take a deep breath, and as we breathe out, we imagine loving energy going out from this opening to the person we are sending the love. We try to send the feeling of love rather than using the word "love." Teachers also recommend avoiding a visual image of the recipient.

After we breathe out while sending love, we breathe in. While breathing in, we imagine love coming to us from all the sentient beings on earth. Other teachers do not include this replenishment step, and a depleted feeling can result. Russell recommends doing this exercise toward a specific person nine times a day for nine days. Other teachers advise doing it for twenty minutes a day for ten days. The exercise is best done outdoors, with the recipient unaware of it.

You will see the more dramatic results where you have conflict, with people with whom you do not get along. Years of estrangements in families have ended, and relationships in the workplace have improved. One man told me that his sister-in-law had a strong dislike of him and the two had hardly spoken in ten years. After doing this relatively simple exercise nine times a day for nine days, he received a pleasant note from the sister-in-law.

Mietek Wirkus has said that this technique also works on animals and plants, and that animals are especially sensitive to being loved. They respond quickly. If you are skeptical, you might do an experiment with two groups of plants. Send love to one group for nine days, and then compare how well the two groups flourish. For a clean experiment, you should have someone else do the watering and care for the plants during the nine days so you don't unconsciously favor one group over the other.

The regular practice of this exercise also helps the sender's emotional development. He becomes a more compassionate person. When senders of love see concrete results, like the man who received a pleasant note from his sister-in-law, they often recognize that our thoughts and feelings have power. Communication between people does not have to be in words.

Chapter Nineteen

The Power of Amulets, Ritual Objects, and Place: Unusual Phenomena and Healing

One of the goals of this book is to show that spiritual yearnings and a desire for healing are cross-cultural and universal. They are not limited to Americans of European descent. In many cultures physical objects and particular places are believed to have spiritual and healing power. Some examples are the power objects of Native Americans, icons in Greece and Russia, and relics throughout both Christianity and Buddhism. A concrete example came up in my private practice.

Celia and Glenn saw me for marital counseling. They had been married for six or seven years and their relationship had been good until the last year or two, when bickering and fault-finding had increased. Progress in counseling was slow until Glenn's job required a brief trip to Southeast Asia. On a free day, while walking through the city, he noticed a beautiful statue of Kwan Yin in a shop window. He bought it. Some call Kwan Yin the Chinese goddess of compassion. Buddhists believe that she is one of those saintly beings that has renounced her own development and chosen to remain on the earth plane to assist sentient creatures until all have reached the goal of enlightenment.

When Glenn returned home, he placed the statue on the bureau in their bedroom. Their relationship changed. Bickering decreased, and each became more thoughtful toward the other. Both had been thinking of divorce, but they decided to stay together. That was twenty years ago. I met them recently, and they are still together and seem happy. What caused the change? Did the statue representing compassion remind them to be more compassionate toward each other, or did the statue evoke the unseen presence of a helpful goddess? Celia and Glenn think it may be a combination of both.

Belief in the spiritual and healing power of particular places is also widespread and occurs in many different cultures around the world. Christians continue to make pilgrimages to Santiago and Muslims to Mecca. Many feel that the boundary between our world and other dimensions is thinner at particular locations. One area with this reputation is the Black Forest. Located in southwestern Germany in the state of Baden-Wurttenberg, the area is about 120 miles long and about 40 miles wide. It is similar to our Appalachians, with five-thousand-foot mountains clothed in forest. The region is saturated in folklore: poltergeists, water nymphs in lakes, ghosts, and a headless horseman on a white steed who roams cemeteries on winter nights.

While hiking in the area, my wife Nancy and I were descending a mountainside when we found a meadow with a statue of a horned demon with red glass eyes. A nearby plaque told of Albrecht, a local man who became lost in the mountains on a foggy night. He encountered a demon, like the one depicted by the statue, who chased him. As the demon gained on him, Albrecht prayed intensely. His prayers were answered when he found a coach on a forest road that picked him up and brought him to his home village.

There is no way of telling whether there is any truth to this story. It could be pure fiction, or it is possible that a local man did become disoriented and lost on a foggy night. Any hallucination due to sensory deprivation would have broken up once the man began running. There would be too much new sensory stimulation from his muscles and his vestibular sense. However, could demons actually exist and come into our world in particular places?

MYSTICAL EXPERIENCES

The most interesting places with special energy are those with a reputation for healing. The history of pilgrimages shows that for millennia, people have known intuitively that some places on earth have a healing energy. There are several excellent books on the topic, but only a few sites where I have had personal experiences are discussed here.

The Star Mounds of Samoa

The Samoan islands are sprinkled with mysterious mounds built of stone without mortar. Most have projections coming off the sides; eight projections are the most common, which led to the term "star mounds." The island of Tutuila in American Samoa has over eighty of these mounds. Some mounds are quite large. Pulemelei Mound on Savai'i, in independent Samoa, is the largest ancient structure in Polynesia. It is forty feet high, and the sides are 160 feet by 200 feet. This required a huge amount of work.

What was the purpose of these mounds? There were several purposes. The first was pigeon catching—not the waddling creature of American cities, but the *lupe*, or Pacific pigeon, a magnificent bird which was prized for its meat. The *matai*, or high chief of each village, would compete with other chiefs in catching the birds, each from the top of his respective mound, with a long-handled net. The winning chief gained great prestige, not just for himself but for his entire village.

Another purpose was social. Each mound was some distance from the home village, and the people prepared large amounts of food in advance. Feasting and partying took place during pigeon catching competitions. During these festivities many of the usual taboos and social restrictions on behavior were lifted, which added to the party atmosphere. Samoan young men continue to use the metaphor "catch a pigeon" for obtaining a girlfriend.

Another purpose of the mounds was worship. Because Christianity became so pervasive in Samoa, it is difficult to obtain information on the earlier religion, but it was animistic. Robert Louis Stevenson spent his last five years in Samoa, where he did some of his finest writing. He became close friends with a Samoan woman who was a devout Christian. She would chide Stevenson when he missed Sunday church services, but much later he learned she also worshipped a shark. It is believed that the mounds with eight projections honor an octopus god, since octopus is an important food in Samoa.

An American graduate student, Claudia Forsyth, discovered the most important purpose of the mounds when collecting data for her Ph.D. dissertation in the early 1980s. She was interviewing a respected elder, who told her:

> Do you know the star mounds? Well, they had to do with the *Taulasea* (healers) and energy and special powers. The ancient Samoans did not build those huge structures and star mounds just to catch pigeons. No sir! They were part of our ancient religion, and so were the *Taulasea* (herbal healers) and the *Taulaitu* (shamanic or spiritual healers). Look into the archeology data on the mounds. The energy is still so strong that it raises the hair on your body just to visit them. I saw a star mound on Savai'i and felt the power which is still there. The whole time I was there, my head felt a pressure on it, producing a feeling that it was swelling.

Scholars began questioning more tribal elders after Forsyth discovered that the mounds were used in healing. They learned that the healers worked in the cleft, the area where a projection met the main body of the mound. The writings of early European and American visitors show they were impressed by the effectiveness of the healers, who often used both herbal and shamanic techniques. The healers were skilled at setting broken bones and treating both injuries and disease. One European visitor thought that death was certain for a man who had been speared in the chest, but the man recovered after treatment by indigenous healers. The visitor noted that one of the few problems where the healers were not effective was severe head injuries from clubs.

While in Samoa, I visited star mounds looking for the feeling of energy that the elder had described to Forsyth. At some I did not feel anything, and my dowsing rods did not move. The spiritual energy must have dissipated in those places. At other sites I had a powerful sensation, similar to sensations I get near a healer; for example, when I visited the renowned American healer Olga Worrell. At those mounds where I felt strong sensations, my copper dowsing rods also became active.

Unfortunately, modern Samoans know little of their early religion, and most are unaware of the location of mounds in their own vicinity. An experienced guide is necessary to get to the mounds, because they have become covered with jungle growth and are quite difficult to find. Even Pulemelei, the largest of the mounds, has jungle encroaching on three sides and a mango tree has sprouted on top, now thriving to a height of more than five feet.

Stone Circles and Ancient Cairns of Britain and Ireland

Ancient stone monuments, remnants of a prehistoric age, dot the landscape across Europe and Asia. They go far north into Scandinavia and to Malta in the south. Koreans have told me that they extend to the east across Asia, and some are in their country. They are particularly numerous in Britain and Ireland. Two counties in the southwest of Ireland, Cork and Kerry, have a combined total of more than one hundred stone circles.

Who constructed these monuments, and why? Archeological investigations have come up with surprising finds that add to the mystery. Previously it was thought that megalithic construction was originally developed in Egypt and Babylonia, and that these techniques slowly spread westward across the Mediterranean and then up the Atlantic coast of Europe. Radiocarbon dating has shown that this notion is false. Some of the stone works of Western Europe—for example, Newgrange in Ireland and Callanish in Scotland—pre-date the pyramids.

The purposes of the stone works are another mystery. One purpose was obviously astronomical observation for farming, an ancient farmer's almanac. The growing season in Northern Europe is short. For example, Callanish, on the Isle of Lewis in the Outer Hebrides, is at a latitude of 58 degrees, less than 400 miles from the Arctic Circle. If a crop were planted too early, a cold spell would kill the seedlings, and if planted too late, there might not be enough time for the crop to bear before the end of the growing season. The problem of planting too late is well known to modern suburban gardeners when they end the season with an abundant crop of green tomatoes that refuse to ripen.

Most of the stone structures mark events on either a lunar or a solar calendar for agricultural planning. At Newgrange in County Meath, the sun peers through a roof box only on the morning of the winter solstice and illuminates the interior for seventeen minutes in a spectacular way. Other monuments mark the solstice sunset, and many mark either the spring or the autumnal equinox. Callanish, also known by its Gaelic name, Calanais, impresses because it has both solar and lunar functions. It marks the summer solstice, the equinox sunsets, and a remarkable lunar cycle. Diodorus Siculus, a first century BC Greek historian from Sicily, believed that the stones of Callanish also marked the rising of the Pleiades. Along the southeast horizon a mountain range called *Cailleach na Mointeach*, or Old Woman of the Moor, looks like the profile of a sleeping woman. Every 18.6 years the moon appears to dance along the form of the woman.

The stones had other purposes in addition to astronomical observations: they marked religious festivals. Planting time for much of Scotland and Ireland would have been 120 days after the winter solstice. Ten days later would have been Beltane, approximately May 1st. Beltane, along with Samhain (pronounced Sou-wen) on

MYSTICAL EXPERIENCES

Nov. 1st, were the two most important religious festivals in pre-Christian Europe.

There was one even more important function of the circles. At Callanish there are two smaller stone circles within sight of the main monument. Construction of those circles must have taken a great deal of work that would have been unnecessary if their purpose was only astronomical observation. The people could see results from the nearby main site. Like the star mounds of Samoa, the stone circles of Europe had several functions, and a major one was healing.

We can infer a healing function of the stone circles for several reasons. Chi or Qi, a biological energy of people, determines health and well-being, but Chi can become congested or blocked. The goal in acupuncture is to restore the flow of Chi, but there are other techniques to restore Chi. The healer Mietek Wirkus and his wife Margaret have conducted workshops on bio-energy. I attended one, and in his workshop we were taught to feel the energy of people with our hands a few inches from the body of the person we worked with.

With a little practice this is an easy task, and we were able to detect the energy field around a partner. In one exercise the energy around my partner felt normal, but there was a feeling of stuck or congested energy around his shoulders. The image of Atlas carrying the world sprang to my mind. I asked Carlos if he had too much responsibility, and he was startled. He was managing a multi-million-dollar project, but since many of the workers were contractors from other firms, he could not give direct orders. He had to go through supervisors at their firms, and those supervisors were often not on site. Carlos was in the difficult situation of having responsibility without authority.

The late Olga Worrell was a remarkable healer. At her healing session I attended, the entire room felt charged with energy. Nate, a friend of Native American descent, also attended one of her heal-ings, and he said that he felt that same kind of energy in the circle after a sun dance. In that ritual sacrifice the dancers dance in the hot sun for three days without food or water. In some versions, they hang from rawhide thongs through their pierced pectoral muscles. Nate said that after the sun dance on a Lakota Sioux reservation, the women, children, and the ill people of the tribe walk through that energy field in the circle for healing.

It is likely that the same thing occurred in the stone circles of Europe. Many of the circles are rather small and would not hold more than thirty people. It is likely that the people of the clan or tribe would process through the circle after healing energy was generated through rituals. The energy can still be felt at some locations.

A line of evidence for healing at the ancient sites is the presence of quartz at many of the ancient monuments. In some stone circles there is a central block of quartz with the top at ground level, one of the stones in the circle may be quartz, or quartz pebbles may be found beneath the site. The stones at Callanish are gneiss with quartz inclusions, and the huge surface of Newgrange in Ireland is covered with tons of white quartz. That stone was brought from the Wicklow Mountains, a distance of eighty miles, a Herculean task thousands of years ago. That amount of effort had to have an important purpose. Could the purpose have been healing?

Quartz, or silicon dioxide, is an abundant mineral, but it has remarkable properties. When mechanical stress is applied, it generates an electrical potential. Quartz clocks and watches use a quartz tuning fork to generate a regularly timed electrical pulse to mark time. It is a component of computer chips, and it would be difficult to have our relatively inexpensive modern computer systems without quartz.

More relevant to our topic, shamans on all the inhabited continents have used hexagonal quartz crystals in healing rituals for millennia. Among indigenous peoples today, shamans include a

MYSTICAL EXPERIENCES

small quartz crystal in their medicine pouch. Many contemporary Americans also carry a quartz crystal. They seek crystals that produce a slight tingling, or a feeling of energy in the left palm when the pointed end is held an inch or two away.

Neolithic pottery drums have been found near some British stone circles, and monotonous drumming at a particular frequency induces a trance for shamans. There is also an association between Wicca, or witchcraft, and shamanism. Margaret Murray has argued that witchcraft is not anti-Christian, but rather a surviving expression of pre-Christian pagan religion. Some academic critics dismiss Murray's claim, and they credit the revival of witchcraft to twentieth-century books on the topic. Those academic critics were unaware of the survival of the wise-woman tradition in rural Europe, which is not associated with books. Dermot MacManus, a close friend of William Butler Yeats, documented this tradition in rural Ireland.

When I was a boy, a friend had an experience that showed wise-women continue to exist, not only in Europe but also in America. My friend Frank had been climbing a tree, fell and broke his arm. His parents were away, and he was being taken care of by his grandmother, who was an immigrant from Italy and could not speak English. That was not unusual in the 1950s, when immigrant communities emphasized learning English by the men because they had to compete in the world of work. Learning the new language was considered unnecessary for women, who stayed home to cook and take care of the children.

Frank's grandmother did not know how to get modern medical help, so she took him to a wise-woman who was especially known for herbal remedies and her work as a midwife. When Frank's parents returned, they were appalled that their son had not gotten proper medical treatment, and they promptly got him to a doctor. The doctor took an X-ray and was astonished because the bone had been set perfectly. Frank told me that the doctor also remarked on the cast the wise-woman had made. The doctor said that it was more than strong enough, but lighter in weight than the casts he made of plaster and gauze.

In any discussion of healing and healers, an important question arises: what happens in the body during healing, especially in energy healing and other alternative medicine healing? José Silva suggested that healing practices normalize cell function. This makes sense. Our bodies have to maintain homeostasis, or balance, because mammals need to maintain a constant internal environment to survive. Many functions must be balanced; for example, our body temperature needs to be constant, and our sodium-potassium balance can only vary a little.

Another example of homeostasis is the amount of inflammation. Inflammation occurs when the immune system is activated, and some inflammation is produced when we are exposed to infection or trauma. Some inflammation is beneficial, a part of defense, since it limits the spread of infection. Too much inflammation is destructive and damages the body. Prolonged excessive inflammation can lead to auto-immune diseases as well as cancer.

Scientists who are open to alternative medicine have suggested an additional possibility that occurs during healing. Our cells need to be specialized or differentiated. Skin cells, for example, are specialized to provide a barrier between our internal systems and the outside world. Some cells in the pancreas are specialized to produce insulin, and cells in the liver are specialized to break down toxins, to cite only a few examples. One reason cancer is so destructive is that it takes over bodily organs with relatively undifferentiated cells, and bodily functions break down without the work of our specialized cells. Some have hypothesized that psychic healing energy may support differentiated cells.

MYSTICAL EXPERIENCES

Measuring the Energy

There are four major energy vortexes in Sedona, Arizona. Their energy feels similar to electromagnetic energy I have felt near large generators. I could feel the energy of each site in my body, just as I can feel Chi during acupuncture, but I was unable get an objective measure. I had brought along an electronic device with a selector switch for measuring either an electrical or a magnetic field. Jason Hawes, who developed the TV show *Ghost Hunters* with Grant Wilson, said that these devices were one of their most valuable tools. However, he is measuring a different kind of energy.

My readings at each vortex site were minimal, lower than at my motel, where computers, TVs, and other appliances produced a low level electrical field. The electromagnetic spectrum is huge. It is possible that the energy of the vortexes is at a frequency outside the range of my device, or the energy may not be electromagnetic. It did not cause the needle in my compass to deflect.

The copper dowsing rods were another matter. I had been introduced to dowsing about twenty years ago by my cousin Pat, who owned a farm. He cut a Y-shaped stick of willow about three feet long, and he showed me the correct grip. When we walked around, the stick became active, with the tip bouncing up and down, at two places. It had been a dry summer, and Pat said that when they had a lot of rain, there were springs at the two places where my stick responded.

Pat also told me of Dennis, another man he had taught to dowse. When Dennis had received his credentials as a high school teacher, he took a contractual job teaching in a semi-arid region of West Africa a bit south of the Sahara. After Dennis completed his three-year contract, the local people tried to persuade him to stay. It was not for his teaching skills, but for his ability to help them find the right place to dig wells by dowsing.

The copper dowsing rods I brought to Sedona seemed to come alive and spun at each of the four vortex sites. I passed the rods around to the five others in my group, and the rods responded for all of us. One woman, Iris, became frightened because they seemed to be moving of their own accord. That reminded her of scary Stephen King stories. Steve, the guide, got the strongest response. When he held the rods, not only did they spin, but they vibrated at a rapid rate. I watched him closely from about two feet away, and his hands and arms were steady. He did nothing to induce that activity. Although many American scientists do not believe in dowsing, it is viewed with respect by scientists in many other countries, especially Germany.

Healing Energy at Sedona, Arizona and the Role of Geology

The energy of the four vortices in Sedona can be felt within a quarter mile of each vortex. One of the vortices, located at Boynton Canyon, has long been considered sacred by four Native American tribes: the Apache, Hopi, Navajo and Yavapai. That particular site is the most difficult to get to of the four, but fortunately the guide had a four-wheel-drive Jeep. As we bounced through a rocky gully, he called that part of the trip "the Indiana Jones ride."

The guide, Steve, was a spiritual man who spent much time with Native Americans in the area. He had participated in their rituals and had been given a tribal name. He encouraged me and his four other guests to sit on the small hill at the Boynton Canyon site for twenty minutes of silent meditation. Local people believe the energy at that site is balanced, and they believe the energy at other sites has either a masculine yang energy or a feminine yin energy.

What causes the energy at Sedona? The area has huge rock formations, some resembling cathedrals, bells and even coffee pots. Various colors are present, but intense reds are most predominant, and they glow in spectacular shades at sunrise and sunset. The rocks are of sandstone, and the brilliant red colors come from coatings of iron oxide over quartz particles. Other minerals, such as magnesium and calcium carbonate, are also present. The core of our spinning planet is a molten mass of iron and nickel. Some speculate that the molten core spins at a different rate than the layers above, and that generates energy. They believe this energy is conducted to the surface by the minerals in the rocks at Sedona.

Does the energy at Sedona produce healing? It certainly feels like it does, but that question cannot be definitively answered without a controlled clinical trial. Locals believe that the energy stimulates creativity. Steve, the guide, agreed with this. He said that after ten years at Sedona, he gave up his full-time job with the National Park Service to have more time for music. Now he works as a guide four days a week and devotes three to music. He both plays and composes, and he has produced one CD thus far. Steve said he had not experienced creative impulses before coming to Sedona.

The Role of Ritual at Sites of Healing Energy

Rituals play a role in the energy of sacred sites. In Japan in the hills a couple of miles from the huge 13th century bronze statue of the Buddha at Kamakura, there is a cave where I saw several people in silent prayer, lighting candles and burning joss sticks. The feeling of spiritual energy was intense. I felt moved, so I also lit some joss sticks and prayed. There is the question of whether that site was a natural energy center, or did the spiritual activities of the people over the years at that location produce energy that was absorbed by the walls of the cave?

There are energy vortices which shamans call power spots at several places in the world. The Snaefellsjokull glacier in Iceland, Mt. Shasta and Sedona are examples. I do not know what it is about the geography of those places that gives them power, but people who visit those sites can feel it. Human activities and rituals also produce power at the sites where they are performed. Some of the great cathedrals of Europe were built on sites that were used by the earlier religion. It is likely that the earlier people chose power spots for their worship and healing rituals. The cathedrals may have the energy of a power spot, plus energy absorbed from the prayers of people who worshipped in the cathedrals.

I have also felt strong healing energy at some of the effigy mounds in the American Midwest. At those places Native American tribes created huge mounds in the shape of animals. Some are so large—for example, the serpent mound in Ohio—that they were not recognized until seen from the air. A mound in the shape of an eagle near Madison, Wisconsin, gave me a particularly strong feeling of healing energy. Wiccans have told me that some of their rituals create healing energy. They cast a circle of a specific size, and then perform rituals within the circle to raise "a cone of power." The cone is healing energy that fills the circle and extends to a single point in the universe high above.

I am reminded of another line of reasoning from the B-grade spy movies of my youth. The protagonists were often told to be careful of their speech because "the walls have ears." In a sense that is true, because all walls have ears. If two people have a conversation in a room, some of the energy vibrations are absorbed by the walls. In traditional, non-system physics, it is believed that the energy simply disappears. Physicists with a dynamic energy systems approach believe that the vibrational energy continues to exist in the wall, and if we had the technology to extract it, we could decipher prior events in that room. I think that we can conclude that the feeling of healing energy at particular sites is due to a combination of natural energy at those locations and energy generated by human activities.

Visiting and examining ancient stone sites is satisfying; it connects us with our remote ancestors. We have also met interesting people during our visits. At a circle in Ireland we met a British couple who told of their trip to Callanish, commenting that some of the stones at Callanish vibrate with energy. Of course that led us to Callanish, and we found that it is true. Resting your hands on some of the stones, it is possible to feel a slow rate of vibration. In Scotland we met some who believed their stone circles were haunted.

There are three well-preserved stone cairns at Balnuaran of Clava in Scotland, which is only a few miles from the tragic battlefield of Culloden Moor. These were built about 4,000 years ago, and the first cairn marks the winter solstice. It is similar to Newgrange, but it is the setting sun rather than the rising sun that sends a beam of intense light to the back wall. We felt strong energy, and the dowsing rods responded to all three cairns. That visit was memorable because the only other people at the site were a pleasant, small group of Wiccan women from Germany. The hood of their car was decorated with a large circled pentagram.

We had an adventure of a different sort when we visited a court tomb, a megalithic tomb with a concave forecourt in County Tyrone in the north of Ireland. After we parked, we had to walk about a half-mile across private agricultural land to get to the site. Most farmers are gracious and allow visitors to cross their land as long as the visitors are careful to close all gates after them; otherwise animals will stray.

On the return to the car we had a problem. Several cows became curious and tried to approach us. This alarmed the bull escorting his "girls," and he began to move toward us in a menacing way. We retreated across a cattle grid, a trench covered with steel bars that animals are afraid to cross. He stood between us and our car, and he kept us there for some time until we waved the cows away. After the last cow left, he quickly followed and we were able to reach our car.

Drombeg in County Cork is one of the more attractive stone circles we have visited. It is a beautiful circle of seventeen large stones, one of them recumbent, or lying on its side. The top surface is flat, which led to the nickname "the Druid's Altar." Some believe that the stone was used for human sacrifices. That myth is false; during excavations the cremated remains of only one human was found at the site. Nearby cooking areas were found, reminiscent of the feasting and partying at the star mounds of Samoa.

The sunset of the winter solstice is marked at Drombeg by the path of the sun between the two entrance stones in relation to the recumbent stone on the opposite side of the circle. This was a difficult feat for ancient people. During the weeks leading up to the solstice, there is very little movement of the sun across the horizon. In the week before and the week after the solstice the sun does not seem to move. The ancients at Drombeg used a cleft in the hills on the horizon to help get it right.

In 1935 a British archeologist, Boyle Somerville, who had studied Drombeg, brought the psychic Geraldine Cummings to the circle. She said that horrible things had been practiced there, including violent dances and blood sacrifices. She said that Drombeg was cursed, and "guarded by the spirits of darkness." Based on this, the archeologist Aubrey Burl advised visitors to "bring garlic, a cross and lots of friends."

When I visited Drombeg with Nancy, a rain was falling, so we were the only visitors. I experienced a quiet feeling of healing energy, and also a strange feeling of sadness. I was reminded of the words of the poet Gary Snyder, who recommended leaving a small offering for the spirits at ancient sites. Snyder said that since spirits are mainly non-material, a little goes a long way. He said, "A thimble full of sake is enough for a banquet in the spirit world." I reached into my daypack and grabbed a small offering, which I put on the Druid's Altar. Immediately I felt bathed in a warm feeling of intense healing energy. There was no feeling of negativity or malevolence.

The isles across the north Atlantic are not the only places where people kept track of the solstice and were concerned with healing energy. At Machu Picchu in Peru there is a ridge about a half mile across from the temple with a stone structure called *Puerta de Sol*, or "gate of the sun." There are openings in the gate that make the sun visible from the temple when it comes over the horizon at both the winter and the summer solstice.

The Importance of Preserving Sacred Sites

We need to preserve these ancient sites. Some sites, such as Newgrange, have been declared World Heritage Sites by UNESCO, but all the stone circles in Britain and Ireland cannot be protected by UNESCO. Twenty-six years ago in County Kerry I examined a modest stone circle. The stones of the circle were small, about twelve to eighteen inches high. Some stones were missing, so the circle was not complete. There was a large block of quartz in the center partially covered with soil, but the quartz peeked through. Despite the modest size, there was a pleasant and mellow feeling of healing energy. On a recent trip I went back to re-visit the site and found a traffic circle in that location. That is a tragic loss.

Steps need to be taken to preserve ancient sites; for example, when the site is on private farmland, the farmer should be given some compensation to preserve the site. The preservation problem is not limited to Britain and Ireland. In the U.S. West I have seen petroglyphs from earlier civilizations that are pockmarked with bullet holes because Americans have used them for target practice. In Morocco ancient rock art has been chiseled off cliffs for sale to collectors. This is particularly selfish and also unnecessary. There are several professional artists who will take a photo of rock art, make a stencil, and sandblast the images onto a sheet of blank rock. It is difficult to distinguish these reproductions from originals.

Occasionally preservation efforts cause inconveniences, but that cannot be avoided. For several years I was on the waiting list to go into the cave at Altamira in Spain, which has magnificent Stone Age cave paintings. Three months before I was to enter the cave, it was closed to visitors. Moisture and nutrients in the breath of visitors were fostering the growth of microorganisms on the walls, which was damaging the paintings.

Mexico has had a long struggle for preservation due to the many artifacts among the ruins of Pre-Columbian civilizations. Mexico has passed antiquities laws prohibiting the export of ancient artifacts, but the smuggling of statues has been a serious problem. At an auction house in the U.S. I was puzzled when I saw an appraiser smell and then taste a statue from Mexico. I learned that some entrepreneurial Mexican men were making reproductions of ancient stone statues and then burying them in manure for two to three years. The harsh chemicals in the manure make the statues look aged after a couple of years.

Mexico is making good progress in its efforts to protect its petroglyphs and cave paintings. People are not allowed to visit cave paintings in the sierras without a licensed guide. The guides go through training and must pass a rigorous test. Hopefully more countries will follow their example. In addition, international agreements are needed to protect the valuable sites that remain. We need laws against trade in rock art similar to the laws against trade in ivory. When we disrespect our ancestors by giving their sacred sites shabby treatment, we are disrespecting ourselves.

Conclusion

The human stories told in this book have shown a spiritual aspect of reality often ignored in the modern era. The experiences of people from prisons to Main Street, as well as other cultures, show that the spiritual world is real and give cause to wonder and explore. If we open ourselves to the spiritual world, we can experience a new realm of the mystery and fun of being human.

Reference Notes

Introduction

Moskowitz, M. (2000). *The power of Kabbalah*. Niles, IL: Nightingale Conant Inc.

Moskowitz, M. and Y. Berg (2003). *The 72 names of God*. Niles, IL.: Nightingale Conant, Inc.

Reston, J. (1971, July 26). Now, about my operation in Peking. *New York Times*.

Chapter One

Fletcher, G. (2009, October). Spirits of the fight: the battle of monocacy has spurred its share of ghost stories, specters, and sightings. *Frederick Magazine*, 40-49.

Freuchen, D. (editor) (1961). *Peter Freuchen's book of the Eskimos*. New York: Fawcett Co., 157.

Mead, M. (1928). *The coming of age in Samoa*. New York: William Morrow and Co., 69-72.

Watkins, P. (2004). *The fellowship of ghosts: a journey through the mountains of Norway*. Washington, D.C.: National Geographic Corp., 136-137.

Chapter Two

Presentation on William L. Mackenzie King (1986). Gatineau Provincial Park, Quebec, Canada.

Stiles, M. (2002). *Yoga sutras of Patangali*. San Francisco: Weiser Books.

Tart, C.T. (1975). *States of consciousness*. New York: E.P. Dutton and Co.

William L. Mackenzie King (2010). Wikipedia.com.

Chapter Three

Ehrlich, G. (2001). *This cold heaven: seven seasons in Greenland.* New York: Pantheon Books.

Eliade, M. (1964). *Shamanism: archaic techniques of ecstasy.* Princeton, NJ: Princeton University Press.

Fiore, E. (1987). *The unquiet dead: a psychologist treats spirit possession.* New York: Ballentine Books.

Harner, M. (1980). *The way of the shaman: a guide to power and healing.* San Francisco: Harper and Row.

St. Claire, D. (1978). *Lessons in instant ESP.* Englewood Cliffs, New Jersey: Prentice Hall, Inc.

Wickland, C. A. (1924). *Thirty years among the dead.* Los Angeles, CA: Llewellyn Publications.

Chapter Four

Baba Ram Dass (R. Alpert) (1971). *Be here now, now be here.* New York: Crown Publishing.

Cooper, D.A. (2006). *Invoking angles for blessings, protection, and healing.* Boulder, CO: Sounds True, Inc.

Chapter Five

Kushner, H. (1981). *When bad things happen to good people.* New York: Harper Collins, Inc.

Chapter Six

Sheldrake, R. (1999). *Dogs that know when their owners are coming home.* New York: Three Rivers Press.

Sheldrake, R. (2005). The sense of being stared at. *Journal of Consciousness Studies,* 12(6), 10-31.

Chapter Seven

Adam (pseudonym). (2003). *Dream healer.* New York: Plume Books.

Harner, M. (1980). *The way of the shaman: a guide to power and healing.* San Francisco: Harper and Row.

Holmes, T. and Rahe, R. (1967). Life stress inventory. *Journal of Psychosomatic Research*, 11, 213-218.

Ingerman, S. (1991). *Soul retrieval: a guide to mending the fragmented self.* San Francisco: Harper Collins.

Radin, D., Taft, R. and Yount, G. (2004). Effects of healing intention on cultured cells and truly random events. *Journal of Alternative and Complementary Medicine*, 10(1), 103-112.

Siva, Sri. 2001. *Personal transformation program.* Niles, IL: Nightingale Conant Corp.

Targ, R. (2004). *Limitless mind: a guide to remote viewing and transformation of consciousness.* Novato, CA: New World Library.

Thompson, A. (2008). The psychology of shamanic healing: An interview with Stanley Krippner. *Shaman's Drum* 78, 17-23.

Chapter Eight

Davis, E.W. (1985). *The serpent and the rainbow.* New York: Simon and Schuster, Inc.

Eastlake, D. (1985). Personal communication.

Elliott, R.C. (1966). *The power of satire: magic, ritual and art.* Princeton, NJ: Princeton University Press.

Mooney, J. (translator) (1891). *Sacred formulas of the Cherokees.* Washington, DC: U.S. Government Printing Office.

Plato. (1970). *The laws.* Harmondsworth, England: Penguin.

St. Claire, D. (1978). *Lessons in instant ESP.* Englewood Cliffs, NJ: Prentice Hall, Inc. pp. 51-52.

Wilson, D.P. (1948). *My six convicts.* New York: Rinehart and Co., Inc.

Chapter Nine

Emoto, M. (2010). *Messages from water and the universe.* New York: Hay House.

Lewis, Jr., D. and A.T. Jordan. (2002). *Creek Indian medicine ways: The enduring power of Muskoke religion.* Albuquerque: University of New Mexico Press, 118.

Targ, R. (2004). *Limitless mind: a guide to remote viewing and transformation of consciousness.* Novato, CA: New World Library.

Chapter Ten

Bem, D.J. and Honorton, C. (1994). Does Psi exist? Replicable evidence for an anomalous process of information transfer. *Psychological Bulletin,* 115(1), 4-18.

Beneviste, J., B. Ducot, and A. Spira. Memory of water revisited. *Nature,* 370(6488): 322.

CNN (1995, Sept. 21). Carter: CIA used psychic to help find missing plane.

Jimserac, C. (2008). The facts about an ingenious homeopathic experiment that was not completed due to the tricks of Mr. James Randi. International Academy of Classical Homeopathy, Alonissos, Greece.

Lindberg, C.A. (1953). *The spirit of St. Louis.* New York: Charles Scribner's Sons, Inc.

Logan, R. (2009). Randi backs out of challenge with homeopath. Nature News.com.

Randi, J. "The Amazing" (2009). Exciting times at the JDEF. http://www.randi.org.

Silva, J. (1994, July 22). Speech at Sheraton Hotel, BWI Airport, Linthicum, Maryland.

Tart, C.T. (1975). *States of consciousness.* New York: E.P. Dutton and Co.

Chapter Eleven

Boone, J.A. (1954). *Kinship with all life.* San Francisco: Harper and Row, Inc.

Houston, J. (2002). *Mystical dogs*, Maui, HI: Inner Ocean Publishers.

Sheldrake, R. (1999). *Dogs that know when their owners are coming home.* New York: Three Rivers Press.

Vogel, V.J. (1970). *American Indian medicine.* Norman, OK: University of Oklahoma Press.

Chapter Twelve

Jackson, K.H. (1971). *A Celtic miscellany: Translations from the Celtic literature.* Harmonsworth, England: Penguin Books.

Lewis, Jr., D. and Jordan, A.J. (2002). *Creek Indian medicine ways.* Albuquerque, NM: University of New Mexico Press.

Mack, J. (1994). *Abduction: Human encounters with aliens.* New York: Scribner's, Inc.

Monroe, R. (1971). *Journeys out of the body.* New York: Broadway Books.

Moskowitz, M. (2000). *The power of Kabbalah.* Niles.IL: Nightingale Conant Corp.

Chapter Thirteen

Campbell, J. (1983). *The way of the animal powers: Vol. 1, Historical atlas of world mythology.* San Francisco: Harper and Row.

Coelho, P. (1993). *The alchemist.* New York: Harper Collins.

Chapter Fourteen

Eliade, M. (1964). *Shamanism: archaic techniques of ecstasy.* Princeton, NJ: Princeton University Press.

Solomon, P. et al. (1961). *Sensory deprivation: a symposium held at Harvard University Medical School.* Cambridge, MA: Harvard University Press.

Freuchen, D. (editor). 1961. *Peter Freuchen's book of the Eskimos*. New York: Fawcet Co.

Weatherup, K. *Practical shamanism: a guide for walking in both worlds*. San Diego, CA: Hands Over Heart Publishing.

Mason, H. (ed). 1970 *Gilgamesh: a verse narrative*. New York: New American Library.

Hart, R. and Reed, A.W. *Maori legends*. Wellington, NZ: A.H. and A.W. Reed, Ltd.

Fitzgerald, R. (translator) 1990. *Odyssey*. New York: Vintage classics.

Hiatt, C. (translator). 1983. *Beowulf and other old English poems*. New York: Bantam Books.

Kinsella, T. 1970. *The Tain: translated from the Irish epic Tain Bo Cuailnge*, London: Oxford University Press.

Mathews, J. 1991. *Taliesin: shamanic and bardic mysteries in Britain and Ireland*. London: Aquarian Press. pp. 14-15.

Whitehead, R.H. and McGee, H. 1983. *The Micmac*. Halifax, NS: Nimbus Publishing, Ltd. Pp.53-55.

Montgomery, C. 2004. *The shark god: encounters with ghosts and ancestors in the South Pacific*. New York: Harper Collins. pp. 82 and 83.

O'Hogain, D. 1991. *Myth, legend and romance: an encyclopedia of Irish folk traditions*. New York: Prentice Hall Press. p. 357.

Perkins, J. 1997. *Shape shifting: shamanic techniques for global and personal-transformation*. Rochester, VT: Destiny Books.

Pryde, D. 1971. *Nunaga: ten years of Eskimo life*. New York: Walker and Co.

Goodman, F. personal communication.

Chapter Fifteen

Chadwick, N. 1968. *Dreams in early European literature*. In Carney, J. and D. Greene (editors), Celtic Studies, New York: Barnes and Noble, Inc. pp. 33-50.

Garfield, P. 1974. Creative Dreaming. New York: Simon and Schuster, pp. 61-62

Landy, D. 1977. *Robert Penn Warren's dream novel: an interview with RobertPenn Warren.* Washington Post, Feb. 25, 1977, pp. B1-B7.

Dwyer, R. 1987. Discussion at International Association for the Study of Dreams, Arlington, VA.

Hall, C. S. 1966. *The meaning of dreams.* New York: McGraw-Hill.

Chapter Sixteen

Janis, S. 2000. *Spirituality for dummies.* New York: Hungry Minds, Inc. p. 143

Freuchen, D.(editor) 1961. *Peter Freuchen's book of the Eskimos.* New York: Fawcett Co.

Stiles, M. 2002. *Yoga Sutras of Patanjali.* San Francisco: Weiser Books.

Wirkus, Margaret and Mietek, *Bioenergy - a healing art.* self published. Derwood, MD.

Miller, G. 1958. The magic number seven, plus or minus two: some limits on our capacity to process information. In Beardslee, D.C. and Wertheimer, M. *Readings in Perception.* Princeton, NJ: Van Nostrand, Inc.